ENTREPRENEURSHIP AND PUBLIC POLICY

Recent Titles from Quorum Books

Entrepreneurship and Public Policy

CAN GOVERNMENT STIMULATE BUSINESS STARTUPS?

Benjamin W. Mokry

QUORUM BOOKS
NEW YORK • WESTPORT, CONNECTICUT • LONDON

Library of Congress Cataloging-in-Publication Data

Mokry, Benjamin W.
  Entrepreneurship and public policy : can government stimulate
business startups? / Benjamin W. Mokry.
      p.   cm.
  Bibliography: p.
  Includes index.
  ISBN 0–89930–239–4 (lib. bdg. : alk. paper)
  1. Entrepreneurship.   2. New business enterprises.   I. Title.
HB615.M65   1988
338.9—dc19   87-24934

British Library Cataloguing in Publication Data is available.

Library of Congress Catalog Card Number: 87–24934
ISBN: 0–89930–239–4

First published in 1988 by Quorum Books

Greenwood Press, Inc.
88 Post Road West, Westport, Connecticut 06881

Printed in the United States of America

∞

The paper used in this book complies with the
Permanent Paper Standard issued by the National
Information Standards Organization (Z39.48–1984).

10   9   8   7   6   5   4   3   2   1

For Phyllis and Chris

Contents

Figures

Tables

Introduction

Entrepreneurship is in a renaissance in America today. People are creating small businesses in record numbers and are receiving an immense amount of attention from policy makers interested in creating jobs and raising incomes. Promoting entrepreneurship has taken its place alongside industrial recruitment as a component of economic development policy, even displacing it in some cases. Before entrepreneurial promotion becomes too well established as the new economic development orthodoxy, we need to consider some basic questions.

How does entrepreneurship occur? Can public policy intervene in the process in a positive way? How is promoting entrepreneurship different from "traditional" economic development? Are there prerequisites for entrepreneurial policy to be effective? Are communities up to the task of designing and delivering the right assistance to the right people at the right time and will it make a difference in entrepreneurial behavior?

Anecdotal evidence exists about "what small businesses need" and about how providing it helped a particular community or collection of firms. A number of writers have discussed specific actions governments should take to help entrepreneurs. Yet it is amazing that many states and communities have jumped on the entrepreneurial bandwagon with so little evidence that assisting entrepreneurs makes any difference in local economic health. The reply "Nothing else is working and such efforts can't hurt" is true to a point, but do we want to travel the same road we did with industrial recruitment incentives? An immense amount of evidence shows that most recruitment incentives, such as tax abatements and cheap loans, make little or no difference in business location patterns, yet state and community continue to act as though they do. Passing complicated legislation and establishing bureaucracies to deliver programs makes up a substantial portion of what we do when we go about "promoting economic development."

Most of the attention to entrepreneurial promotion to this point has been taken up with the care and feeding of the program delivery mechanisms, such as venture capital pools or business incubators. Should we blindly copy model entrepreneurial programs without carefully examining what will be accomplished once they are in place?

This book is one effort to address these concerns but it is not intended merely to challenge the use of entrepreneurial promotion policies. It is primarily directed at making more intelligent use of this approach. We need to understand the business startup decision before we can design effective policies. Entrepreneurs are unlikely to pay attention to the political climate or government incentives unless these policies are sensitive to the way the entrepreneur sees the world. I hope this work stimulates economic developers, policy makers, and citizens interested in their community's future to think more critically about the assumptions behind current efforts to promote entrepreneurship and economic development. I do not conclude with a "new and improved version" of development policy. Development policies must be designed by local people in light of local resources, market gaps, and needs, and I give the reader something to ponder while undertaking this effort.

ENTREPRENEURSHIP AND PUBLIC POLICY

Small Businesses and Smokestacks: Opportunities and Challenges for Development Policy

HARNESSING ENTREPRENEURSHIP FOR ECONOMIC GROWTH

The 1970s were a traumatic time for the U.S. economy.[1] The Keynesian premise that central governments can maintain economic growth through macroeconomic and fiscal policies was sorely tested. Government, business, and labor alike came in for growing public scorn because they appeared unable to boost the economy's sluggish performance or reduce inflation. Government seemed incompetent and costly. U.S. firms appeared inefficient, unresponsible, and complacent compared to foreign competitors, especially the Japanese. Unionized workers were seen as self-serving and unwilling to adapt to new competitive pressures. Public confidence in these institutions declined throughout the 1970s and remained low even after the economy began to expand again in 1983 (Lipset and Schneider 1987).

The entrepreneur, symbol of individualism and mysterious link between idea and product, has gained visibility as attention began to focus on innovation, competitiveness, and productivity. Articles and books appeared reporting on the entrepreneur or telling how to become one (Vesper 1983; Drucker 1985). New magazines, such as *Inc.*, cover and serve this portion of the business community. Entrepreneurship is taught on college campuses, and in rural areas it is pursued as a solution to economic distress (MDC, Inc. 1986). The entrepreneur has become something of a talisman and symbol of hope for the American economy as it moves into the twenty-first century.

While entrepreneurship is glamorous, creating a small business and making it successful is hard work. Untold numbers of business ideas never see the light of day, although some could well be profitable. Many of the small firms that are started fail within their first few years. Failure is part of the market system; not everyone has a good idea for a business. But are existing businesses startup and failure rates fixed? Difficulties in getting a business under way or making it successful may simply be attributed to a poor product but could be due to weak business skills, insufficient capital, or an unrefined idea, problems that might be avoided with careful preparation and a supportive environment.

This presents a dilemma for economic development policy in the U.S. One of the foremost champions of the private sector, Ronald Reagan, reflected the thinking of many Americans when he said private enterprise and market forces could easily fulfill the public's wants if only government would get out of the way (Salamon and Lund 1984). One effect of this view is a reluctance to fund existing domestic programs generously, much less undertake new ones. As much as President Reagan and many Americans want to believe that economic health depends on just freeing individual initiative from government intrusion, this is not the complete story. In fact, it may be impossible for entrepreneurship to fulfill its promise in today's economy without government supports and incentives.

America is developing a policy toward entrepreneurship but it is being shaped by state and local governments, not at the federal level. Between 1981 and 1986 fifty of the federal government's major grant-in-aid programs, including those for community development, housing, and Appalachian development, were reduced by more than 50 percent in constant dollars (AFSCME study 1986). State governments between 1984 and 1986, meanwhile, more than doubled their average spending on economic development and are undertaking increasingly sophisticated development policies. States now combine traditional domestic industrial recruitment and financing with international marketing and recruitment, university–business linkages, targeting of industries and areas, and nourishing entrepreneurship with technical assistance and venture financing (Pilcher 1986; Clarke 1987; Epstein 1987; Balderston 1986).

This is a study of one aspect of the entrepreneurial phenomenon, the business startup rate,[2] and its relationship to public and private efforts to create a supportive environment for entrepreneurs. The narrow question to be examined is whether local economic development efforts influence the startup rate of new businesses. Evidence on this will come from counties in New York, Pennsylvania, Ohio and Michigan. More than an exercise in program evaluation, however, the study also offers a theoretical framework for understanding the channels through which government policies affect entrepreneurial behavior. Despite the rash of policies intended to help entrepreneurs that have emerged in the last few years, surprisingly little attention has been given to exactly how entrepreneurs attend to government policy as they scan their environments for information. Several questions will be considered. In what ways might government policy affect entrepreneurial thinking? Can such policies be designed and managed at the community level? How effective are such policies in influencing entrepreneurial behavior? These issues will be taken up in the following chapters. In the rest of this chapter, we will examine the contribution of small firms to the U.S. economy. We will also examine traditional development policies and briefly contrast them with policies often recommended to help small firms.

THE SMALL FIRM AND JOB CREATION

In 1985 the number of business incorporations reached 668,904, a record level and a 5.3 percent increase over 1984. Business starts stood at 119,065, an increase of 16.4 percent, the largest increase since 1980 (U.S. Small Business Administration 1986, 2–3). The birth, growth, and market exchanges of small firms are major sources of economic change. Small firms are more inventive and produce jobs at higher rates than larger firms in the United States. One study of seven industries estimated that small firms created two to three times as many innovations per employee as large firms (Gellman Research Associates, n.d.). Moreover, small firms have generated large numbers of jobs in slow-growing sectors of the economy and in older industrial areas of the North and Northeast (Armington and Odle 1982).

Three features of businesses are important in understanding the contribution of small firms to job creation: the size of firms adding new jobs, the age of the fastest growing firms, and whether they are independents or not. In recent years small enterprises with less than 100 employees comprised about 33 percent of total U.S. employment and about 32 percent of total U.S. sales (SBA 1984, 12–13).[3] In the 1980–1982 recession, however, these firms produced more than their share of birth- and expansion-generated jobs. This can be seen in Table 1.1.

Small firms added about 39 percent of the birth-generated jobs and 47 percent of the expansion jobs. Large firms created larger absolute numbers of jobs but lost more jobs due to deaths and contractions than they created. On balance *all the net new jobs added to the economy between 1980 and 1982 were added by small firms.*[4] Small firms seem to perform well in periods of expansion also. Industries dominated by small firms (less than 500 employees) posted an average job growth of 5.1 percent while industries dominated by large firms averaged a 0.7 percent job growth in 1984–1985 (SBA 1986, 6). In a study of St. Joseph County, Missouri, Sue Birley found that company birthrates were stable during expansions and recessions, and that the job creation rate (2.9 percent per year) and loss rate (1.75 percent per year) were very stable as well (1984).

Young firms produce most of the new jobs. David Birch (1979a) found that, for the country as a whole, firms under five years old produced approximately 80 percent of the new jobs created between 1969 and 1976. Firms in older age groups produced much smaller percentages of new jobs: ages five through eight (9.4 percent); nine through twelve (6.0 percent); thirteen and above (5.2 percent) (1979a, 19).[5] A study in California found

Table 1.1
Components of Job Generation Change 1980–1982 (thousands of jobs)

	Total	Births	Deaths	Expan.	Contrac.
All Estabs.	982	9,354	-11,171	10,224	-7,425
Small Est.	2,650	3,610 *(38.5)	-3,416 (30.5)	4,803 (46.9)	-2,347 (31.6)
Large Est.	-1,668	5,744	-7,755	5,421	-5,078

Source: U.S. Small Business Administration. The State of
Small Business: A Report of the President Transmitted to
the Congress, March 1984 (Washington, D.C.: U.S. GPO), 27.

Note: Small Firms are those with less than 100 employees.
Small Firms employed 34.1% of all workers in 1982.

* Percentage which small firms contributed to component of
change.

that firms under a year old added employees at a much faster rate than more
established firms (Greene 1982). Work by Teitz, Glassmeier, and Svensson
(1981) also supports the notion that younger firms produce most of the new
jobs.

   Recent evidence suggests that in rural areas small independent firms are
less effective at creating new, stable jobs than multi-establishment firms
(Miller 1985). Nevertheless, firms that are small and independent have a
great potential to produce new jobs, and rural areas are being encouraged
to focus on developing local businesses since other approaches are not working well. Birch examined the net job creation experience by size and organizational status of establishments between 1969 and 1976.[6] He found that
independent firms with less than twenty employees by themselves produced
almost 52 percent of the net new jobs created in this period. Middle-sized
and large firms produced relatively few net new jobs. Birch also found that
small, independent firms produced all the net new jobs in the Northeast,
and for the South, West, and Midwest, they produced 54 percent, 60 percent,
and 67 percent of the new jobs respectively. Erdevig (1986), using a different
data set, found that in the Midwest, births and expansions of small firms
were more important than contractions and closings in explaining the rate
of job creation over time. In fact, locations with the highest birth and
expansion rates also tended to have high failure rates.

   In light of his data, Birch observed:

The findings suggest that it makes little sense to attempt to influence firms to move
(in the physical sense), nor is there much opportunity, short of influencing the

business cycle, to influence the rate at which firms contract or go out of business. Practically all the leverage lies in affecting where new firms locate and where existing firms choose to expand. (1979b, 16)

This is the most telling reason for assisting small new firms. Small firms create many new jobs and probably could do better since they face many obstacles. In contrast to the newfound hope in the potential in helping small firms, there is increasing skepticism about the staple in economic development: industrial recruitment.

INDUSTRIAL RECRUITMENT

Most economic development practice builds on a simple version of export base theory (Bearse 1976, 37–38). The characteristics of this approach are, first, a belief that manufacturing is the sector on which development efforts should focus, especially where it exports products out of the local economy. This brings "new money" in and supports suppliers, business services, and retail operations. Manufacturing earnings are "multiplied" in the local economy, while services merely "take in each other's wash."

Second, economic developers try to compete for the branch or relocation of large, stable employers, preferably those that promise to bring in hundreds of jobs at once. Advertising campaigns, mailings, and prospecting trips to growing areas figure prominently in these efforts to capture the attention of outside investors. In the past, recruiters traveled to Illinois and Massachusetts while today the trips are to Japan, Korea, or Taiwan. The purpose is the same, however—to entice a branch plant into the state or community.

A third characteristic is to focus a great deal of attention on tax rates and the kinds of taxes levied in different states. Standard development theory accepts that politically controllable factors (tax policy, incentives, services) are of secondary importance in location decisions. Markets, location, raw materials, labor, and transport costs are the primary factors considered. Yet it is held that it is important for governments to maintain a good "tax climate," i.e., to offer tax incentives, because this is one of the few tangible things governments can do to show business that the area cares for them.

Finally, economic developers rely heavily on subsidized debt in assisting business. Industrial revenue bonds or government-backed bonds are featured prominently in the arsenal of development tools. Because selling revenue bonds depends on the ability of the firm to repay, local capital assistance usually goes to stable, established firms with a credit record. Investment decisions of government finance agencies differ little from those of banks, as a result, and in fact government bodies must work closely with banks in funding projects. At best this merely gives firms with good credit an unnecessary break on interest payments, at worst it misuses government's ability to operate somewhat outside market constraints to support projects with long-term payoffs.

These four features of development practice can be found operating in most development agencies around the country. Numerous studies have found that these efforts do little to attract new business to an area or bring about new production.

Tests of the effectiveness of these policies use one of four approaches—case studies of the tax burden faced by a "typical firm," questionnaire studies of businessmen who have made location selections, benefit-cost analyses, and statistical correlation studies—all of which have turned up very weak relationships between the presence of incentives and higher rates of business investment. The logic of tax studies is that firms will flee high-tax states for low-tax havens. Businessmen and governments do not behave in such a simpleminded manner however.

Tax Case Studies. While substantial interstate differences in business taxes do exist, neighboring states seem to keep their taxes in line with each other. This is significant because businesses choose between regions on the basis of what are called primary location factors, e.g., market, transportation access, wage rates, or other input costs. Once a region is selected, specific sites are examined and here policy variables, including state and local tax rates, may be considered (Due 1961; Stinson 1968). So at the point when taxes come into play, the differences are too small to be a major factor in choosing between locations. In 1967 the Advisory Commission on Intergovernmental Relations (ACIR) compared the growth rates of high- and low-tax states and concluded:

Because the tax differentials are so small, it is possible to draw the negative conclusion that there is no clear cut relationship between the level of business taxes and manufacturing employment growth rates for states within the same region. (ACIR 1967, 66, quoted in Cornia, Testa, and Stocker 1978, 11)

The failure of industrial attraction incentives to create jobs is explained by examining the kind of subsidy tax abatements offer. These programs attempt to lower the cost of doing business, especially the cost of capital. But state and local taxes are an insignificant business cost. The Federal Reserve Bank of Boston estimated that the average U.S. business paid 4.4 percent of its income in state and local taxes. Only 1.9 percent went to local property taxes and 0.9 percent to corporate income taxes. A factor reducing the value of local property tax abatements is the fact that part of the value of the tax abatement will be capitalized into the price of the property (Vaughan 1981). Thus the property owner, rather than the business, receives the benefit of the abatement. The question that states should ask is whether the leverage ten-year abatements give them is worth the lost revenues that could be going to improved services.

Questionnaire Studies. If we ask businessmen to name factors they considered in locating where they did, they rarely place government incentives very high. Unless prompted with a list of location factors, including tax and financial incentives, businessmen often point to other factors first.

Vincent Apilado studied the use of Industrial Revenue Bonds (IRBs) in Michigan over a period of five years and found that in almost every case where an IRB was used, firms said they would have made the same location choice without the bond assistance (Apilado 1971). A study of IRB use in Alabama found that of fifty-four firms using them, only one-third would have located outside Alabama if IRBs were not available. More interesting is the fact that 90 percent of the firms in the study located or expanded in Alabama after turning down offers of IRB assistance. Most preferred to own their facilities outright rather than lease them from a quasi-governmental body (Alabama 1970).

Benefit-Cost Studies. Several studies were designed to find out whether there is a net benefit (measured by change in state personal income) to a state if it offers tax and financial incentives to firms. Sazama attempted to take into account differences between the social costs of foregone investment and consumption. Examining data from five states, Sazama found that all benefit-cost ratios exceeded one and ranged from 1.2 to 43.2 over an array of indicators (Sazama 1970, 385).

Another study found that benefit-cost ratios exceed one even if as little as 25 percent of the wealth created by new economic activity stayed in the local area and only five percent of the tax exempt investment took place because of the exemption. When 10 percent of tax exempt investments are induced and new value added retained in the local area is 100 percent, benefit-cost ratios rise as high as 8.78 (Morgan and Hackbart 1974). In other words, tax exemption programs are beneficial to local governments even if only a portion of the benefits accrue to the local area and relatively small numbers of projects actually required subsidized capital.

It is important to be precise about the kinds of firms responding to incentives. Absolute increases in aggregate income could occur at the same time per capita income declines if low-wage industries and low-wage migrants are attracted (Sazama 1970). Industrial revenue bonds are most effective in inducing manufacturing investment. Financial incentives have the greatest impact on capital-intensive industry, not on mobile, labor-intensive firms (Stober and Falk 1969). Labor surplus areas may not see unemployment decline much if the firms they attract are capital intensive. There is a trade-off when aid programs are used to attract investment to locations with high unemployment. Firms attracted to such locations are often ones facing shrinking national markets, rather than high-growth ones. Even if employment is increased through such efforts, governments run the risk of bringing in unstable jobs that are sensitive to national economic swings (Hellman, Wassal, and Falk 1976).

Statistical Studies. Some studies attempted to determine if measures of economic development are correlated with variables such as tax and incentive policies, once urban population, wage rates, and other factors are controlled (Cornia, Testa, and Stocker 1978, 15). Regarding tax concessions, John Due concluded:

On the basis of all available studies, it is obvious that relatively high business tax levels do not have the disastrous effects often claimed for them. . . . However, without doubt, in some instances the tax element plays the deciding role in determining the optimum location, since other factors balance. This is most likely to be the case in the selection of the precise site in a metropolitan area. (Due 1961)

Putting the findings succinctly, Leonard Wheat observed in his 1973 survey of available research, "This (the tax hypothesis) is perhaps the most tested of all hypotheses. And the results of prior testing do not encourage further tests" (Wheat 1973, in Cornia, Testa, and Stocker 1978, 15).

Statistical studies of financial incentives do not reach such neat conclusions. The loan program of Pennsylvania and the revenue bond program of Kentucky did appear to induce new investment. A loan guarantee program in Connecticut was ineffective however (Hellman, Wassal, and Falk 1976).

ENTREPRENEURIAL DEVELOPMENT

The relatively recent insights into the importance of small business have raised sharp doubts about traditional "smokestack chasing" economic development policies. State and local economic developers have come under increasing criticism for too often concentrating on the "blockbuster deal," while ignoring the less dramatic job creation possibilities in smaller, less visible firms (Doctors and Wokutch 1983; Litvak and Daniels 1979). Incentives, such as industrial revenue bonds and tax abatements, are criticized for being too heavily skewed toward larger firms. States compete with each other to offer the most generous aid to business, which some writers see as a fruitless effort to re-create the cost and regulatory constraints of a quarter century ago in order to compete with lower-wage locations in the United States and overseas (Bearse 1976). A different approach to economic restructuring is needed and small firms are expected to play a key part in it (Clarke 1987; Vaughan, Pollard, and Dyer 1984).

Responding to these criticisms, state and local governments are rapidly adapting what will be called here an "entrepreneurial model" of economic development policy.[7] It assumes that new small firms have a large and untapped potential to improve the health of local economies. To take advantage of this potential, state and local governments must themselves become entrepreneurial by adopting risk-oriented, innovative, and flexible ways of helping new firms start and grow.[8]

The distinction between traditional development tools and those focusing on entrepreneurship is summarized well by Malizia. *Growth theories*, e.g., export base or trade theory, take economic structure as given and "focus on short-term changes in the economy and its moves from one equilibrium to another. The quantity of production, consumption, income, and employment or trade is important." The proper role for government is to increase the rate of growth and create more local employment by expanding existing capacity. Government would not be concerned about changing the structure of the local economy. *Economic development theories*, e.g., entrepreneurship or dependency theories, focus on how the economic structure of an area changes in the long run. Structural change includes change in industry mix, product mix, occupational mix, patterns of ownership and control, firm size and age, technologies in use, or degree of competitiveness. "The quality of production and the distribution of consumption are emphasized." Policy's role in this framework is to alter the capacity of the economy to produce in the future (Malizia 1986, 490).

It is economic development theory that excites small business supporters. Albert Shapero illustrates the logic behind this view when he asserts that self-renewing communities with long histories of adapting to events have the qualities of "resilience, creativity, initiative-taking and, above all, diversity."[9] Shapero believes an entrepreneurial climate creates these qualities. If we are interested in renewing older industrial centers, or in maintaining a strong economic base in any community, we should concentrate on

new and developing firms . . . [on] diversity and reduced dependence in any community or region on one or a few sectors of economic activity . . . [and on] creating the ecological conditions conducive to new company formations. (1981, 20)

CONCLUSIONS

These ideas are exciting. They seem to offer a new way of approaching local economic development that is neither a zero-sum game of smokestack chasing nor dependent on federal management of macro-economic policy. The entrepreneurial model implies that local communities are the breeding ground of entrepreneurship and are capable of creating an environment favorable for it. Despite the newfound excitement about small business's contribution, the federal government has not established new programs to assist small business, except in specialized arenas, such as procurement set asides. In fact the Small Business Administration and other federal economic development programs were initially targeted for elimination by the Reagan administration, and their budgets have fallen in real dollars over the last six years. Moreover, the federal budget for economic development is unlikely to grow substantially in the near future. As a result, entrepreneurial policies are being pursued with real vigor only at the state and local level. To this point, however, there has been little consideration of how state and local governments have implemented these programs and how closely they adhere to the outline of activities thought to be necessary to support entrepreneurs. Little research has been done on whether these policies, once implemented, actually have an impact on the startup or survival rates of businesses in the area.

Entrepreneurship offers promise and a challenge to America. High levels of entrepreneurship and risk-taking are vital if the country is to remain competitive in a rapidly changing world economy. Yet entrepreneurial behavior is still an unknown quantity. Can it flourish only by being left alone? Can it be managed so that it generates innovations in large and small firms? Should we try to encourage startups and improve the survival rate for small firms in places where the economy is weak or declining? Will any public policy instruments influence entrepreneurs in ways that will promote public goals, such as job creation or increased incomes? How successful will we be in trying to consciously harness entrepreneurship for economic growth?

Before we can answer these questions we must know more about the entrepreneurial process and more about the ways that government policies might interact with the entrepreneur's way of doing things. This issue is taken up in the chapters to follow.

NOTES

1. This research was partially funded by the U.S. Small Business Administration under grant SBA–8541–AER–84.

2. In this study the startup rate is defined as the number of new businesses started in a county per 1,000 employees in the industry in which the firm was started. Support for this choice of measure is given in Chapter 6.

3. In discussing job generation, enterprises must be distinguished from establishments. Enterprises are independently owned and operated. They may be multipart organizations, i.e., having headquarters, branch, or subsidiary components. Establishments are the smallest unit in which business activity is conducted and for which employment data is collected. Establishments may be a component of a larger firm. It is important to make this distinction because independent small enterprises do not have the same access to credit and management support that components of larger firms might have. Because their needs differ, public policies to assist them would differ as well (SBA 1982, 40).

This research is focused on business entrepreneurs who either start up a new independent enterprise or are operating one less than five years old which he or she started. In most cases, the firms included by this definition have fewer than twenty employees. This usage focuses on small new enterprises and those that are not subsidiaries or otherwise controlled by a larger corporation. This is an intentionally restrictive definition that will exclude much of local economic development policy from being classified as "entrepreneurial" even though it helps small establishments. This is done in order to concentrate on the most entrepreneurial sites, those that help the small independent firm.

4. Similar findings are reported by Birch (1979a) for the 1969–1976 period. Armington and Odle (1982) found that job creation by small firms was proportional to their employment share in the 1978–1980 period. The contribution of small firms to employment creation seems to be affected by the business cycle.

5. These figures are for simple totals of new jobs created, not net new jobs, i.e., jobs lost to deaths or contractions are not taken out of these calculations. Birch provides no figures on net job creation by age.

6. Components examined were: headquarters, branch, subsidiary, and independent enterprises.

7. (Aulde 1980; Balderston 1986; Morrison n.d.; New York State Assembly 1980; New York State Science and Technology Foundation 1983; Pierce and Steinbach 1981; U.S. Congress 1978; Vaughan 1986.)

8. Describing this model as entrepreneurial refers not only to the fact that small, new firms are the targets of assistance but also to the nature of government's behavior. To be entrepreneurial, governments and economic developers must adopt new ways of thinking and acting.

9. Jane Jacobs presents an extended argument supporting this view in *Cities and the Wealth of Nations* (1984).

Chapter 2

The Business Startup: Issues in Designing Local Stimulus Policies

While our knowledge about entrepreneurship is growing rapidly several questions remain before we can design policies to effectively increase business birth and survival rates. Why do some individuals go into business while other people with similar characteristics do not? Is the ability of a person to start a business due more to idiosyncratic factors, such as whether or not he believes he controls his life, or to environmental variables, such as the availability of investment capital? Can government increase the likelihood that individuals in an area will go into business by trying to improve the "climate for entrepreneurship" in the area? Or should government focus its resources on supporting individual businesses once they are started? Exactly how is it that we expect government policy to influence the level of small business activity in an area? Recent research on entrepreneurship will be used to answer these questions and to identify opportunities for policy intervention.

CREATING A POSITIVE CLIMATE FOR ENTREPRENEURSHIP

Criticizing the theory that entrepreneurs can be identified by certain traits, Aldrich and Zimmer jokingly observe that when the number of people who have expressed an interest in starting a business is added to those who actually attempt it, "well over half the population must possess entrepreneurial traits" (1986, 5). If this is true, then the question is, why do so few people ultimately go into business?

Business birthrates (new firms as a percentage of existing businesses) averaged between 9 and 13 percent across U.S. census regions in recent years (SBA 1983). Similar rates have been found in Europe (Aldrich and Zimmer 1986, 8). These "natural" rates of small business births reveal that a fairly

Figure 2.1
Desired Impact of Development Policy on Business Birthrates

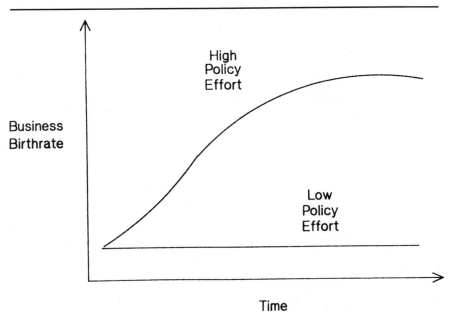

constant but not extremely large proportion of individuals act on their entrepreneurial urges at any one time.

One of the objectives of entrepreneurship assistance is to increase business
startup and survival rates, whatever the natural rate might be. This is illus-
trated in Figure 2.1.

The assumption is that the more aggressive governments are in providing
assistance to entrepreneurs, the more likely it is that individuals will view
the area as a good place to do business. People on the verge of starting a
firm, but who face roadblocks, might be encouraged to go ahead if local
interests are working to improve conditions for small, young firms. But
where should government focus it efforts?

THE STARTUP DECISION

To be useful as a tool for economic development policy, we need a theory
of entrepreneurship that *explains* entrepreneurial behavior and how it comes
about. Variables used to explain the startup decision should include some
that are *manipulable* by means available to government. Research on entrepreneurship is beginning to address the first need but has some way to go
before it will meet the second.

Efforts to understand the entrepreneur cut across several disciplines, including economics, psychology, sociology, and anthropology. Available theories can be classified as trait-based, economic, and contingency.

Trait Approach

An early explanation of entrepreneurship was that some individuals possess traits that cause them to seek out entrepreneurial opportunities to a greater extent than others. Over the years the list of characteristics has grown but includes: alertness, aggressiveness, intelligence, internal locus of control (belief that the individual is in control of what happens to him), low aversion to risk, and high need for achievement. Empirical work suggests that these characteristics do set entrepreneurs apart from the general population. Regular business managers share many of the same traits, however. Why are they not more entrepreneurial? Another difficulty with the trait approach is that traits do not seem related to whether the entrepreneur is successful or not (Gartner 1985, 699; Begley and Boyd 1986). Aldrich and Zimmer (1986) criticize the trait approach for the same reasons that the trait explanation of leadership has failed. No consistent pattern of characteristics explains why certain people emerge as leaders or entrepreneurs in given situations. They argue that situational factors are critical in causing individuals to behave in entrepreneurial ways (1986, 8). Even though personality factors do not by themselves determine entrepreneurial activity, they do seem to predispose people toward leadership in business.

Economic Actor Approach

One of the oldest lines of analysis describes entrepreneurial activity as a function that takes place in growing economies. Hebert and Link, in their excellent review of the literature on this approach, conclude that two concepts linking most economic theories together are uncertainty and innovation (1982). Some scholars (Richard Cantillon, Frank Knight, and Ludwig von Mises, for example) view the entrepreneur's role in dealing with uncertainty as his critical contribution. Others (Joseph Schumpeter, Max Weber, and Werner Sombart) view the entrepreneur primarily as an innovator, with Schumpeter calling him the force behind the process of "creative destruction" that serves as the engine of capitalism. Several scholars (Jeremy Bentham, Arthur Cole, for example) view the entrepreneur as responding to uncertainties in the marketplace through some abilities he may have to create new innovations to better serve demand. Finally, scholars such as Israel Kirzner and John Bates Clark focus on the entrepreneur as perceiving opportunities caused by gaps or mismatches in supply and demand. The entrepreneur helps restore economic equilibrium by organizing resources to supply a need.

A key insight offered by Hebert and Link is that disagreements about the entrepreneur's true economic contribution are unnecessary because uncertainty and innovation are closely related. Entrepreneurship has two faces, "one that reveals itself when the level of inquiry deals with an explanation of change, the other when investigation concerns itself with the effects of change" (1982, 111–12). People behave in an entrepreneurial way not only by inventing new products and processes, thereby causing change and uncertainty, but also by taking advantage of change and uncertainty in order to supply goods or services at a profit.

While the economic approach is useful in understanding the entrepreneur's contribution to the economy, it does not help us understand what types of individuals will act in entrepreneurial ways. The economic approach gives little attention to the entrepreneur as an individual or to his surroundings. By removing the entrepreneur from his social setting, economic theories are not useful for identifying who we should try to help by government policy.

Contingency Approach

An approach now gaining support explains entrepreneurship by combining personal, economic, and sociological variables. This emerging perspective holds that entrepreneurial activity results from the interaction of individual characteristics, turning points in individuals' lives, background and cultural factors, and exposure to examples of success. The product of entrepreneurship is an organization that uses resources and must supply goods or services that others want to consume and will pay for. Management decisions made by the entrepreneur or his team are critical to the organization's survival and growth.

A number of scholars have attempted to bring order to the rapidly growing literature using this approach.[1] A model of the key variables and relationships is suggested by Figure 2.2.

Psychological Makeup. Personal characteristics, such as need for achievement, locus of control, risk-taking propensity, beliefs about wealth and material gain, and business growth, are related to a person's predisposition toward business leadership (Gartner 1985, 702). Belief that the person can influence his destiny (internal locus of control) distinguishes entrepreneurs and managers from the general population (Brockhaus and Nord 1979; Jennings and Zeithaml 1983, 417–18). Entrepreneurs and managers display significantly greater need for achievement and tend to tolerate more ambiguity than the general population (Sexton and Bowman 1984; Schere 1982).

Under certain conditions the psychology of the entrepreneur can even affect the performance of the firm. Gasse found that the entrepreneur's attitudes form a cluster of related values about important business characteristics. He identified two ideal types, managerially oriented and intuitive-entrepreneurial,[2] and found that managerially oriented owners tended to use

Figure 2.2
Factors Shaping Entrepreneurial Activity

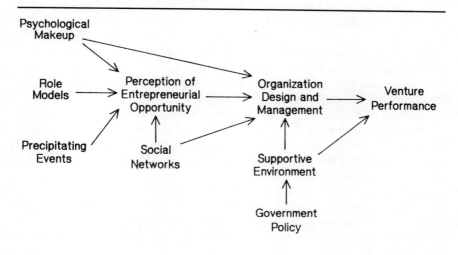

more formal organizational techniques, use more sources of information in making decisions, and in one industry (shoes) create faster-growing firms (1986, 57–58). Other studies confirm that attitudes of owner/managers about their preferred lifestyle, type of work they find rewarding, attitude toward organizational growth and security all affect whether firms grow rapidly or not (Peterson and Smith 1986; Vesper 1980). It is not uncommon for an entrepreneur to find that the firm grows to the extent that it no longer matches his or her preferred operating style. Wise individuals sell out or bring in someone with the appropriate managerial skills. Others fail to act and the firm flounders and perhaps fails (Braden 1977; Govindarajan 1984; Pfeffer and Salancik 1978). The more established the firm, the less important is the owner's personality in determining the performance (Begley and Boyd 1986).

Role Models. Previous work experience and models of entrepreneurial individuals also influence the decision to take the entrepreneurial path. The family is important in making it seem desirable for a person to form a business. Various studies report that over 50 percent of company founders in the United States had parents who were company owners, free professionals, or farmers, despite the fact that these self-employed people made up less than 12 percent of the population (Shapero and Sokol 1982, 84). Individuals who have had experience in a small company, or have themselves previously started a firm, are much more likely to found a new company (Johnson and Cathcart 1979).

Precipitating Events. An "entrepreneurial event" increases the chance that a person will take up entrepreneurship.[3] Shapero and Sokol contend that most individuals are held on a given life path by patterns of forces in their lives, e.g., family, job, or inertia (1982, 79). Powerful changes can push individuals off their established paths into entrepreneurial activity. Among the changes that can do this are "negative displacements" such as forced migration or losing one's job. If there is no chance in continuing in one's previous occupation then the search for new activities becomes much easier. Immigrant populations, such as Cubans in Florida, are responsible for large numbers of new businesses.

Less severe displacements also trigger new business formations. A study of 109 entrepreneurs in Austin, Texas, found that 65 percent mentioned negative factors that led to their startup: being fired, company changed hands, transferred but did not want to leave city, or no future in the job (Shapero and Sokol 1982, 80). Other forced endings can also promote entrepreneurship, such as getting out of the army or school, which Shapero and Sokol describe as being "between things." Positive pulls also cause people to begin businesses. Technical or professional people sometimes find themselves in business after being offered a contract from a client or a partnership with someone (1982, 82).

Some ethnic groups are also prominent in small business formation; Shapero and Sokol cite Jews, Lebanese, Ibos in Nigeria, and Chinese-Americans in the United States (1982, 85; see also Kent, and Sexton, and Vesper 1982; Kilby 1971). Aldrich and Zimmer criticize the simplistic view that particular cultures are more entrepreneurial than others, pointing out that ethnic groups seen to have high business startup rates as immigrants display no special business skill in their homelands (1986, 7). The key point is that marginal groups, whatever the cause of their marginality, have few options and turn to independent business or trade to survive. Ethnic groups, when they become immigrants, are faced with new challenges in a new setting where entrepreneurship becomes an attractive option. Even more to the point, individuals in their native setting can also be put in situations that make starting a business an attractive option. It is then that we see the importance of environmental and situational factors.

Supportive Environment. To explain why the entrepreneurial path is chosen from among the many alternatives open, Shapero and Sokol (1982) suggest that individuals have perceptions of the desirability and feasibility of owning a business. *Desirability* deals with values that are shaped by culture, family, peers, and important others. Shapero and Sokol maintain that a "social system that places a high value on innovation, risk-taking, and independence is more likely to produce entrepreneurial events than a system with contrasting values" (1982, 83). Estimates of the *feasibility* of the entrepreneurial path are shaped by the presence of financial support, models showing that other similarly (or less) gifted people have started and succeeded in business, and mentors, peers, or partners who can help the business succeed. Feasibility interacts with desirability. One may believe that forming a company is infeasible and therefore conclude it is undesirable. If starting a firm is perceived as undesirable, its feasibility may never be considered (1982, 86).

The forces at work in the environmental setting are quite complex as can be seen by looking at three important features of local economic environments: ecological structure, agglomeration economies, and resource base. (Pennings 1982b)

229   The term ecological structure derives from an analogy with the human ecology model developed by Hawley in his 1954 *Human Ecology* (Hannan and Freeman 1977; Pennings 1982c). Much as animal or plant species mutate to fill ecological niches, organizations are viewed as arising in niches where resources, constraints, and opportunities intersect (Aldrich 1979). The organization will be most successful when its structure, technology and resource demands fit the constraints of its chosen niche. Empirical work supports the view that ecological structure influences the rate at which organizations are born into a population (Fennell 1980). In particular the birth of new business organizations is related to the following:

- Size of the human population
- Diversity of organizational population
- Large number of small firms in the area
- Population change
- Ethnic or cultural diversity

Startups tend to be located close to major population centers because that is where markets are most accessible. Entrepreneurs emerge most often from firms smaller than 250 employees, and locations with higher proportions of small firms in related industries show higher rates of startups than locations lacking such characteristics (Johnson and Cathcart 1979). A business population made up of many small firms offers more "incubators" to generate potential entrepreneurs, and more examples of successful startups for the would-be entrepreneur to copy. A growing human population and ethnic or cultural diversity add to the ferment and openness that support entrepreneurial efforts (Pennings 1982b; Shapero 1981).

Large organizational populations also lead to *agglomeration economies* which add to the profits of small firms locating nearby (Webber 1972). Suppliers and specialized business services are available that make it easier for small firms to get the services they need without having to search for them or provide them in-house. This lowers their costs (Kilby 1971). Part of the uncertainty that handicaps the truly ground-breaking startup is reduced for later followers because of the network of supporting organizations that is in place. Business incubators are an attempt to mimic some of these advantages by grouping small firms together in a common facility.

Finally, the *resource base* of the area plays a part in establishing its "carrying capacity" for organizational populations. Ready resource availability is commonly associated with the following elements (Bruno and Tyebjee 1982, 302):

- Entrepreneurial subculture
- Venture capital availability
- Technical labor force
- Incubator organizations
- Universities
- Regional loan policy
- Regional zoning policy
- Supporting services

Other factors diminish an entrepreneur's resources, some of which are controlled by state and local governments. Contributing to the costs of doing business are:

- Tax structure
- Cost of credit
- Insurance costs
- Access and distance to suppliers
- Land cost
- Cost of energy
- Cost of transportation
- Cost of living

Perceptions of feasibility are shaped a great deal by the availability of financial support. Most of the financing for new startups comes from personal savings and borrowed funds, family, and friends. Ethnic groups sometimes form revolving loan associations to support new business, such as Chinese immigrants to the United States using a traditional institution, *hui*, as a way to finance startups for community members. The availability of such financial networks helps maintain high rates of business startups in immigrant populations (Shapero and Sokol 1982, 86).

The availability of capital for buildings and equipment and working capital for inventory, payrolls, and inputs are central problems universally cited by small and new businesses. Capital in kind, such as physical space in incubators, financial packaging advice, as well as direct equity or loan programs are ways of expanding the resource base by freeing up firms' private sources of funds to do other things. Public policies to expand local resources are particularly valuable when they are used to change the risk preferences of

Figure 2.3
Organizing a New Venture: Task, Technology, and Structure

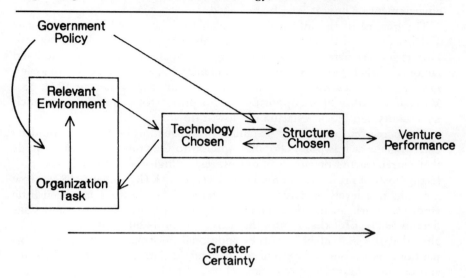

private investors or lenders by lowering the exposure in risky but potentially valuable projects or firms. To serve this function, public funds must not reproduce the biases of commercial lenders or investors; they must choose projects and funds that would not be funded by private sources alone.

Empirical studies of the importance of ecological factors are still rather sparse (Wholey and Brittain 1986). One study covering three detailed manufacturing industries in seventy urban areas found business births were positively associated with the following: human population size and rate of change, occupational differentiation, industrial differentiation, industry size, capital availability, and bank concentration (Pennings 1982b). Marrett found that the availability of organizational models had a positive impact on founding rates (1980). Lincoln found that the presence of certain kinds of voluntary organizations tended to encourage other voluntary organizations to form (1979). Interestingly, instability and turmoil, whether caused by political (Carroll and Huo 1986) or rapid technological change (Brittain and Freeman 1983), seem to free up resources and make it possible for more organizations to be started.

Organization Design and Management. Designing a self-sustaining organization involves solving three problems: the entrepreneurial problem, the engineering problem, and the administrative problem (Randolph and Dess 1981) (see Figure 2.3). The entrepreneurial problem involves choosing the organization's task, i.e., the product or service to be provided. Once the task is chosen it is possible to identify competitors, market opportunities, legal constraints, inputs needed, and scale of resources needed. Uncertainty at this point is high because it is not clear what makes up the relevant environment or how it is to be managed.

The quality of the information available to the would-be entrepreneur and his or her use of it can affect the amount of perceived uncertainty. Uncertainty is here defined as lacking information about environmental factors and their likely impact on the organization and an inability to assign probabilities to events with any degree of confidence (Duncan 1972, 38). While uncertainty offers opportunities for profit (Kirzner 1979), too much uncertainty can block a startup or slow it down.

The perceived probability of failure is a major hurdle for the would-be entrepreneur at this point. Popular opinion to the contrary, research finds that entrepreneurs do not seek out especially high-risk undertakings, preferring instead projects with moderate levels of risk (Brockhaus 1982). How are moderate levels of perceived risk attained? While there has been little empirical work on the determinants of perceived risk (Dickson and Giglierano 1985), Brockhaus notes that perceived probability of failure may be altered if the individual "acquires additional information about the competition, the amount of capitalization required, [and] the managerial skills and technical knowledge required" (1982, 48).

Social Networks. Informal support networks have been found to provide this kind of information in high technology startups (Cooper 1971). Networks may be important to entrepreneurs in other ways (Aldrich and Zimmer 1986). Network contacts can help translate vague ideas about a business into action. Contacts may spur the entrepreneur by providing funding, moral support, labor, a necessary skill, or a shared risk. One study found that individuals who become entrepreneurs often develop complex, loosely structured networks long before they start a business. After forming their business, individuals in the study spent an average of 5.6 hours per week developing contacts and 5.5 hours per week maintaining them. Entrepreneurs estimated that 50 percent of their contacts were unknown to each other. These networks were diverse, encompassing family, friends, co-workers, past employers, bankers, lawyers, and others (Aldrich, Rosen, and Woodward 1986). It is the performance of these informal and private support networks that entrepreneurial policies would seek to stimulate through public or joint public-private action.

The engineering problem involves selecting a technology to accomplish the tasks identified (Figure 2.3). Technology is defined as "the application of knowledge to perform work," i.e., how the organization's work is accomplished. This could be as mundane as choosing office space or as complex as choosing a marketing strategy.

Choosing the organization's structure is critical because there is a relationship between organization performance, structure (how authority and responsibilities are distributed), environmental characteristics, and technology used by the organization (Burns and Stalker 1961; Gillespie and Mileti 1977; Ford and Slocum 1977).

At this point another component of uncertainty identified by Brockhaus may interfere with the startup, the perceived consequences of failure for a specific venture (1982, 48). As figures on equipment, facilities, and labor are firmed up, the size of the personal and financial commitment becomes clearer. The size of the costs may discourage promising investments because capital markets make it difficult for entrepreneurs to spread their risks. Or the entrepreneur may go ahead with insufficient capital and fail.

IMPLICATIONS FOR GOVERNMENT POLICY

The appeal of complex contingency theories is that they encompass most of the factors that seem to affect the startup process. As evidence testing this approach builds, we are seeing more clearly the complex, variable, and uncertain setting in which government policy must operate.

In this setting government policy makers have essentially three choices. They can try to increase the supply of potential entrepreneurs. Efforts can be made to increase the ratio of active to potential entrepreneurs. Assistance can be provided during the birth and early life of the business to increase the chances that the firm will survive. All three approaches are important and are in fact being addressed to varying degrees by many states and communities. However, the variables influencing behavior in the three settings and the nature of the tools available to government make it most difficult to increase the supply of entrepreneurs and most feasible to try to help businesses survive. Increasing the ratio of active to potential entrepreneurs is not impossible but more difficult than simply helping firms that are already off the ground.

Creating a more entrepreneurially oriented population requires that fundamental characteristics of the society be systematically altered. In the short run (and probably in the long run as well) the ability of conscious public policies to change basic human orientations and preferences about business is extremely limited. Cultural values about business ownership, risk, and lifestyle would need to be oriented to support business ownership to a greater extent. In the United States the attitudinal support for these ideas is already extremely high. History, education, and myths all shape these values and are very difficult to change by means of conscious policy. Some of the variables affecting entrepreneurial orientation, such as family business background and psychological makeup, are idiosyncratic. It is extremely unlikely that government policy can do much to substitute for them on a widespread basis. This has not stopped some communities and school districts from trying. Free enterprise education and mentor programs are but two examples of efforts to instill the entrepreneurial spirit in people. While such programs make organizers feel good about themselves, it is doubtful the programs do much to increase the supply of potential entrepreneurs in the aggregate.

The challenge of increasing the efficiency with which society turns potential entrepreneurs into active entrepreneurs has to do with affecting individuals' perceptions of risk and feasibility of business ownership. The fact that the person is thinking about business ownership means that the issue of desirability is settled and the question is whether a viable business idea and organization can be developed. Promoting this stage of the process requires a focus on social networking, information about markets, consumer preferences, technological breakthroughs, and production or process improvement needs. Information flowing between people from diverse backgrounds increases the chances that someone with a different perspective will see a market gap, the possibility of applying a process or product in a new way, or improving an activity in a way not perceived by other people. Science and technology parks and university-business collaboration, the dissemination of patent information, and commercialization of government research are examples of this approach in practice. Improving the flow of information is an especially legitimate function of government policy and is unlikely to have critics.

The third focus, assisting emerging businesses, is in line with traditional small-business assistance and is a well-established policy arena. We would not increase the supply of entrepreneurs but the survival of those who actually begin a firm. Assisting entrepreneurial businesses is different from helping established small businesses and traditional industrial recruitment, however. Public investments are riskier, the forms of assistance more challenging to design and administer, and the payoffs longer term than governmental actors are used to.

Government actions may affect startup processes in a more indirect way. Addressing managerial weaknesses, information gaps, and political climate may change would-be entrepreneurs' perceptions about their business idea and about a particular location as a place to do business. Governments may be able to increase startups by intervening at this stage. Government policy may also influence the startup process at the point where technology and structure are being chosen. Policy can influence technology-structure relations through its impact on the scale of the operation and on the sophistication of the fit between organization and its environment. For example, scale might be influenced by the availability of cheap money for buildings and equipment. Policy might also leverage enough private money to permit a more sophisticated organization to be created.

Cooperation and shared responsibility between state and local policy makers and organizations is critical if any of these efforts are to succeed. Many of the factors influencing entrepreneurs are manifested at the community level, and local knowledge is needed in designing policies sensitive to the entrepreneurial opportunities that emerge. There is no way to develop the support networks that seem to be needed without bringing in community involvement. But community resources alone are insufficient. Proposing that governments greatly increase support for small firms must take into account the cost and complexity of servicing this client group. Consider the multi-billion-dollar investment governments have made over many decades establishing research and delivery mechanisms in agricultural extension. A significant thrust to assist new businesses demands a similar long-term investment in community-level structures. Anything less is merely symbolic. These considerations make us very humble about how much we can accomplish in helping entrepreneurial processes.

POLICIES TO ASSIST ENTREPRENEURS

What would a set of entrepreneurial and risk-oriented policies look like? Writers urging such policies on governments typically recommend that they address four issues that plague the startup firm: access to capital, management, information on supplier and buyer markets, and the political climate facing small firms. The first adds to an area's resource base while the second and third increase the range and quality of information available to the firm. The last deals with perceptions of government.

Capital. As used here capital is defined by two components: financial resources and physical space. Equity or equity-like financing is the preferred financing mechanism for new firms, but proponents of government intervention say financial markets do a very poor job of moving equity funds to entrepreneurs (Kieschnick 1979; for challenges to this view see Charles River Associates 1976; Tassey 1977). Studies show that only about 5 percent of all possible investments are ultimately funded by venture capitalists (Johnson 1979). As a result few small firms use this means; the overwhelming majority of new ventures are begun with personal savings, with some also using financing from friends and relatives, and commercial bank loans (Daniels and Kieschnick 1978; Fenstermaker 1972). New firms are almost always undercapitalized and heavily indebted from the start.

State governments and their localities have a number of avenues open to them for making more equity funds available to new firms: setting up Small Business Investment Companies (SBICs), providing state guarantees, brokering deals linking investors with firms, or direct public investment (Kieschnick 1979). Other ways of increasing the flow of venture capital include:

1. Permitting state employee pension funds to invest in venture capital pools.
2. Creating tax incentives to encourage more private investors to move into venture capital.
3. Using tax monies or bond proceeds to set up a risk capital pool to be managed by a private company or quasi-public agency. (Special Report 1983)

Forms of equity financing that could be provided include four standard instruments: common stock, preferred stock, convertible debt, and subordinated debt. Examples of each have been used in various states and communities around the country (Kieschnick, Litvak, and Daniels 1980; Jarret 1979; Hansen 1979).

The Massachusetts Technology Development Foundation was started with a grant from the U.S. Economic Development Administration and the Commonwealth of Massachusetts. Since 1978 it has invested $3.4 million in over twenty companies and has leveraged more than $20 million in private monies. New York, Indiana, and Michigan have begun similar venture capital pools in recent years (Special Report 1983; New York State Science and Technology Foundation 1983). The Connecticut Product Development Corporation is interesting in that it provides equity by buying part of a company's product when it is at the development and pre-marketing phase. The firm agrees to pay the Corporation a royalty on profits it may earn from the product (Bearse and Konopko 1979).

Capital assistance also takes the form of helping firms locate physical space appropriate to their needs. The availability of low-cost space close to markets has been found to attract small firms to urban areas (Carlton 1980; Daniels and Kieschnick 1978; Gudgin 1978; Pennings 1982b). One mechanism to do this would be to develop small firm incubators by either refurbishing existing space or by building completely new facilities. The government would subsidize overhead and operations costs for items such as utilities, photocopying, secretarial services, and janitorial needs, thereby freeing the founders to take care of research and development, production, and marketing.

Along with space, the facility may provide assistance with business and organization management problems faced by young firms. Some localities concentrate on the technical services needed by new firms without actually housing the firms together in a facility. Efforts in Houston Texas seek to connect accountants, lawyers, and business service suppliers with new firms for no or low initial cost. The key is the technical support rather than the location ("Incubator Without Walls" 1986).

As the incubator concept matures, governments are finding that simply having a facility and technical support is not enough. Once firms graduate from the facility they face the same financial and market problems any small firm in the area would. Illinois, which has many incubators in smaller rural towns, is trying to help firms by marketing products and services from incubator firms as a group. Incubators located near each other will eventually coordinate their efforts around marketing to particular urban areas or supplying different parts of the same product ("Increase the Odds" 1986). Other strategies for using incubators include expanding business ownership among traditionally disadvantaged populations and speeding the commercialization of new technologies (Mt. Auburn Associates 1986).

The objectives behind establishing incubator facilities would vary from place to place. In highly populated places with high rents the availability of small spaces at subsidized rates might be especially critical. In rural areas, cooperative efforts to increase market penetration might be more important. Ideally, the need for incubators and other forms of assistance targeted to small firms should become unnecessary if an area's climate for entrepreneurship is enhanced to the point that it is able to spin off new firms on its own at high rates.

Efforts to assist small firms are evolving very rapidly in terms of the depth of support provided, program spending, and expectations about impacts. It is critical for policy makers to consider what they want from the program and to monitor the implementation. Questions that must be answered include: what type of incubator will fit local needs, how should it be funded and where will funds come from, how will the incubator be managed to produce results, and what criteria should be used to determine the success of the approach (Mt. Auburn Associates 1986, 10).

Management. Addressing management weaknesses is another way governments could promote the birth and survival of small firms. Managerial weaknesses are a principal reason that small firms fail (Kieschnick 1979, 57). One survey of investors dealing with small firms found that most small firms fail because of difficulties in one or more of the following areas: production (technical know-how), marketing (planning and executing sales program), financial management and controls, and organization structure and management depth (Johnson 1979, 80). A report issued by the National Governors' Association in 1983 recognizes the importance of increasing the information available to entrepreneurs.

Technological innovation is driven by entrepreneurs, not by money, government, or universities. State strategies for the promotion of technological innovation, business development and economic growth are incomplete if they do not directly address the critical need for entrepreneurial training and support. (Quoted in Special Report 1983, 7)

Governments could provide assistance through in-house staff or could contract with businesses or academic units to provide managerial and technical assistance for a low fee. Management assistance might be combined with financial packaging, and assistance in marketing, sales, or regulatory matters to give the firm a full range of assistance in one location for "one stop shopping" (Private Sector Initiatives 1979). More firms may be started if entrepreneurs see such programs as lowering their perceived chances of failure.

Information. Market data is another difficulty small firms face. Governments could broker important transactions that individual firms only rarely engage in: locating appropriate business services (lawyers, accountants), identifying market opportunities, arranging long-term financing, or selecting sites for expansion (Schmenner 1980, 57). If governments develop the expertise to competently perform such activities, it not only expedites businesses' operations but also improves the image of the government in the eyes of businessmen.

Political Climate. This is a concept with objective and subjective components. Governments concerned about economic development attempt to project what they think is a favorable image toward business. Incentives are offered, advice provided, regulations changed, facilities constructed or revamped, and advertising put out, the usual goal being simply to show that the area is a good place to do business. Another aspect of the objective side of political climate is the kind of firm that receives assistance. Common categories are outsider firms looking to relocate or establish branches, or established firms in the community. Governments convey information to the business community when they choose to help some firms while seeming to ignore others.

How these actions are received by businessmen is the subjective component of political climate. Businessmen are often prepared to think negatively about government (Bozeman and Bozeman 1987), primarily because of tax and regulatory actions. Even when government tries to help firms, the image of non-business bureaucrats and paperwork make businessmen unwilling to bother with government or trust what it does. Since governments must tax and regulate in order to provide services and protect human welfare, an apparently insoluble conflict is created. No matter what services or incentives governments provide to some businesses, they cannot eliminate the conditions every business must deal with: taxes and regulations. The result is that governments are criticized as never doing enough. Writers often assert that the nature of a community's policies creates a "business climate" that promotes or stifles investment (Bryce 1979; Butler 1981; Downs 1978; Heikoff 1979). As used here, climate is defined by two features. First, it means the willingness of governments to work with business. Roger Schmenner observes,

Tax and financial incentives may be insignificant factors in actual location decisions, dwarfed even by more basic public policies, but their design and marketing may, in fact, be effective indicators of community willingness to work with industry. . . . The community that actively disdains such incentives, especially the more mundane programs affecting location, may do so at its peril. (1980, 463–64)

A second aspect of climate is the kind of business activity that government legitimizes (Aldrich 1979; Meyer and Rowan 1977; Meyer and Associates 1978). Until very recently, local economic developers ignored small, new firms of less than twenty employees. Gollub and Waldhorn point to the opportunity for local governments to significantly influence their business climate by what they call "non-service approaches," which means using

policy tools (such as regulation and deregulation, tax policy change, and administrative reform) in new ways and on defining new roles for key public and private
actors (through collaboration with the private sector, promotion of self-help, and
public advocacy) rather than on direct service delivery (expenditures based on tax
revenues or Federal grants). (1980, I–7)

Non-service approaches include changing inspection procedures to be less
burdensome, establishing ombudsmen, undertaking advocacy for small firms
with insurers, capital sources, and government bodies, targeting public infrastructure improvements to coordinate with private sector self-improve-
ments, or investing public funds with banks that are making greater efforts
to lend to local small businesses.

Reducing regulatory burdens is a non-service approach that has received
special attention. The 1980 White House Conference on Small Business
highlighted regulatory reform along with improved access to capital, improved managerial assistance, and greater involvement in public policy as
four of the six priority areas of concern to small business (U.S. Congress
1980). Governments could actively promote new firm formations by reducing regulatory requirements on very small firms, studying the impact of
regulations on small firms before making rules, setting up "one-top" permit
offices, and taking as much of the burden off the small-firm owner as possible
(Bearse 1976; Private Sector Initiatives 1979; Schmenner 1980). Even where
states and localities do not control the rule making, providing ombudsman
services would be a useful and visible adjunct to other development efforts.

SUMMARY

The easiest solution for a policy maker who wants to promote entrepreneurship is to get elected in a place where natural entrepreneurial activity is
already well established. The startup process is complex and the policy tools
available to influence it are few and frustratingly crude. Physical buildings,
financing, information, and supportive attitudes are things that governments
can offer, but these fail to reach the fundamental forces that cause entrepreneurship to come about. Policy to assist entrepreneurship will need to
be flexible, targeted to gaps in market processes, proactive, and imbued with
a long-term perspective that patiently waits for results. Unfortunately the
environment in which economic development policy operates rarely shares
these characteristics.

In lieu of promoting higher levels of entrepreneurship, governments may
want to focus on making the balance of conditions in an area more favorable
for people in the pre-startup and active startup phases of their businesses.
We are then not trying to create entrepreneurs but helping small businesses,
a task that we know more about. If such policies actually influence individuals' behavior, one basic effect should be an increase in the rate of business

startups. Determining whether policy differences produce this effect requires that we compare sites that have adopted more entrepreneurial policies to sites that have adopted fewer of them. This is the subject to which we turn in the following chapters.

NOTES

1. For elaboration see Long and McMullin 1984; Carsrud, Olm, and Eddy 1986; Hart and Denison 1987; and Gartner 1985.

2. The outlook of "managerially oriented" businessmen would be characterized by organization, planning, professionalism, rationality, and the predictive management processes. The "intuitive-entrepreneurial" businessman would have a perspective characterized by enterprise, opportunism, individuality, and intuition.

3. Entrepreneurial events are characterized by: initiative taking, consolidation of resources, management of the organization created by its founders, relative autonomy of organizational decision makers, and risk taking where the organization's success or failure is shared by the founders. Such events may occur in business or government, new and small organizations or old and established ones, and through the acts of continuously creative individuals or those for whom entrepreneurship is a one-time act (Shapero and Sokol 1982, 78).

Chapter 3

Promoting Entrepreneurship Locally: There Is a Will But Is There a Way?

We have seen that features of the community setting are very important in producing entrepreneurial activity. The presence of an entrepreneurial culture, a diversity of organizations, resources, and information networks are some of the features of the local landscape that influence entrepreneurial activity. If public policy is to be effective, it would have to build on existing community features supportive of entrepreneurship. Community involvement from the public and private sectors is critical if this is to come about. In this chapter we consider the ability of communities to act in this entrepreneurial way.

ECONOMIC DEVELOPMENT: THE ONLY LOCAL ISSUE

There is an interesting incongruity in the literature on local economic development. It is thought to be important that government take the lead in developing public-private partnerships. Voters are said to evaluate local officials in part by how the local economy performs. And economic development is widely recognized to be a primary concern of local political leaders. If this is the case, the following analysis by Garfield-Schwartz makes a great deal of sense.

Cities vary greatly in the success of their economic development efforts. The variation may be explained more by sociopolitical factors than by economic factors. If we could measure success along two dimensions, one the number of large enterprises, the second the degree of integration of the business, labor, and government power structures, we might find that... success in economic development varies with the coefficient of integration. Clearly, in cities where voters evidence a strong anti-business bias, or where fragmentation of the business community or severe labor-management antagonisms exist, local governmental efforts will be severely hampered. (1979, 161–62)

At the same time, Garfield-Schwartz emphasizes that local policy is limited in what it can accomplish, "Macroeconomic forces dominate the performance of the urban economy. . . . A given locality's economic performance is conditioned by both national and regional growth cycles" (1979, 161). Regional shifts in factor cost advantages and population explain most of the boom in the Sunbelt and the slow growth in older industrial regions. Moreover, local governments are constrained by state laws that define their powers. Are local governments even capable of responding to the high expectations voters and economic development scholars foist on them?

While the direct effects of state tax and financial incentives on business investment are fairly small, policies are symbolic gestures that may cause firms to look at one location more favorably than another. Image building is a game at which locals can play too. Shapero's "environment for entrepreneurship" is to a great extent an effort to create the impression that a particular area is a good place to begin operations. In some cases this may be nothing more than providing highly visible financial support to small businesses, tracking down information and disseminating it, or supporting the interests of local firms with state or federal bodies (Gollub and Waldhorn 1980).

The startup decision differs from the decision process used by a multi-unit company to locate a site for a new facility. The startup decision is geographically bounded to a greater degree than the plant location decision. The large company will first select the broad region of the country where it will locate and then examine specific sites in that territory. Most entrepreneurs start new firms where they are living and working, never considering other parts of the country (Cooper 1971). The choice the entrepreneur makes is not between locations, but between starting the firm or not starting it at all (Gudgin 1978).

A number of variables thought to be important in the startup decision, such as migration or the richness of organizational networks, are beyond the control of local governments. Others, such as the amount of capital flowing to young firms, the availability of information and low-cost sites, might be influenced by local governments (Malizia and Rubin 1985). In short, because entrepreneurs rarely look much beyond their own backyards, local policy may "make a difference" (Pratter and Niles 1980) to individuals who are considering setting up a business.

Note also that interest in nurturing development in local areas is likely to be highest among private and public groups at the local level. Williams and Adrian found that economic development was one of the principal preoccupations of policy elites in the cities they studied (1963). Economic development was one of the two key dimensions used to distinguish localities in Eulau and Prewitt's analysis of local policy processes (1973). Molotch (1976) and Peterson (1981) argue that city politics is primarily concerned with how to promote growth and maintain the economic base of the city.

There is, however, a good deal of variation in the level of effort and degree of sophistication of local development efforts (Pelissero 1986; Lewis and Tenzer 1985).

Local groups certainly are likely to have the interest and may be able to effectively channel resources to improve the environment for entrepreneurship whether alone or in concert with state, federal, or private entities. The question is, how effectively can they carry out their critical role in entrepreneurial promotion?

MANDATES AND LOCAL AUTONOMY

Suggesting that local governments might carry out entrepreneurial development policies brings up an issue that has held the interest of intergovernmental relations scholars for a number of years. That is, how much autonomy local governments are likely to have vis-à-vis the states. The powers of locals may be so constrained by state legislatures that they cannot act in an entrepreneurial way even when they want to.

A key limitation on the autonomy of municipal governments (here including county, city, town and village governments) is Dillon's Rule (Zimmerman 1983). Handed down by Justice John Dillon in 1868 it states that municipal corporations owe their origin to, and derive their powers and rights wholly from, the legislature. Later he held that "any fair doubt as to the existence of a power is resolved by the courts against the corporation." Judicial rulings over the years have expanded the interpretation of state interests to include most matters with which municipal governments might be concerned. The result is that locals cannot take the initiative without prior approval of state legislatures (Zimmerman 1981a).

Municipal governments were not always so limited. The scope for local action was very broad until the 1850s. The heyday of railroad building found many cities making investments in lines that promised to make them centers of commerce but that ended in default. An element of Progressive thought is evident in Dillon's ruling in that it attempts to protect taxpayers from politicians desiring to invest public monies in risky projects (Frug 1980).

An examination of contemporary state-local relations shows that even today there is great variation in the amount of autonomy states give their local governments (ACIR 1982, 1981a, 1981b; Stephens 1974). Yet there has been a consistent trend toward more centralization of the decisions on key matters, such as structural form, personnel matters, and financing. The main causes have been increased pressures for equalization of school funding, property tax limits, and increased use of state revenue sharing to cover expanded municipal responsibilities and shifts in taxable property from central cities to suburbs (Zimmerman 1981a). In addition, mandates have increased over the years in areas such as employee pensions, welfare services, and education (Lovell 1981).

These findings would seem to indicate that there is little purpose in studying local economic development actions because all the important decisions
are determined by legal and political forces external to the community. This
conclusion is wrong for two reasons. First, it overlooks flexibility that local
governments enjoy within their relations with higher-level governments.
And second, it ignores important differences between standard governmental
functions (on which autonomy studies have focused) and economic development programs.

Local Governments: Autonomous Dependents

Attempting to measure local autonomy can produce anomalous results.
New York State, for example, has taken an interventionist approach vis-à-
vis its local governments. The state constitution grants home rule powers
to localities, yet in practice few actions are beyond the purview of the state
legislature. Surveys of local autonomy place New York in the lower half of
states on rankings of amount of discretion given to local governments (ACIR
1982, 1981b). Along with its oversight, however, the state channels about
60 percent of state tax revenues to local governments, the highest level of
support of any state in the country (Zimmerman 1981b, 339). On this
ranking New York comes out as being very decentralized in its state-local
relations.

Evidence from a forty-eight-state study indicates that the state share of
state-local revenues has increased since the 1950s, which has been accom-
panied by increased state aid to local governments (Stonecash 1985). States
that provided more services directly at the beginning of the period did not
significantly increase direct spending (some even decreased direct service
delivery), while states that were initially highly decentralized in program
delivery became more centralized. However, increased reliance on state
revenues by local governments does not necessarily translate into less autonomy for them in making policy decisions. A high level of state support
gives localities financial resources and flexibility that simple measures of
state mandates, state spending, or legal powers would not detect (Stephens
1974). Studies of policy implementation point out that local govenments are
effective partners in determining what the "policy" is since they help decide
how to spend the money locally (Bardach 1977; Lipsky 1980). In policy
arenas as diverse as housing, employment and training, education, and water
resources, it is not unusual for supervising agencies in higher-level governments to enforce program guidelines weakly in order not to offend needed
local constituencies (Massey and Straussman 1985).

The multiple funding sources available for economic development give
local governments flexibility in assembling "packages" to carry out local
goals, even when these needs are not precisely met by any one state or
federal program. The result is that while discretion appears to be highly

constrained by state constitutions and formal allocations of powers, significant local autonomy exists.

Economic Development: A Unique Government Activity

Economic development is unlike other government services. One difference has to do with the absence of state-mandated programs or procedures, unlike the situation found in many other public services. There is no requirement that local development bodies exist or offer particular services to the business community. Economic development is a "permissive" activity in that local governments are subject to state or federal rules only when they choose to use state or federal funds. Economic developers can use particular development tools or ignore them as they choose. Meaningful differences therefore exist in the level and type of economic development policy that is pursued in different locations.

A second factor contributing to variation in policies and level of effort is that organized development promotion takes place in private or quasi-public bodies, often in conjunction with governmental activities. Moreover, economic development issues are non-routine in nature and there is no ready "technology" for solving them (Rubin 1985, 1). Usually, the directors and staff of organizations, such as Local Development Corporations (LDCs) and Chambers of Commerce, consider themselves private entities and may resent being identified with government. Even public bodies, such as Industrial Development Authorities (IDAs), enjoy a good deal of autonomy despite operating under state and federal legislation. Developers in some locations can be acting in very entrepreneurial ways while those in other locations do not.

The degree of local autonomy can be assessed in terms of two issues. Flexible funding is extremely crucial if local bodies are to engage in any significant development activity. Are the resources available in the intergovernmental system for them to use for economic development purposes? A second issue is the number of strings attached to the funds. There are no categorical grants for promoting entrepreneurs, so if local developers want to help small firms they must find programs without strings or programs that can be adapted to their purposes.

TOOLS FOR POLICY ENTREPRENEURSHIP

Local economic developers usually have a "well stocked candy store" available to them (Gray and Spina 1980). The most common programs used by developers are reviewed below, starting with those accessible to local development corporations. Programs available in New York State will be used as examples. New York is extremely active in creating incentives but comparable programs can be found in most states.

Table 3.1
Typical State Business Development Incentives

Source and Type	Characteristic	
	Constrained	Permissive

State (Fiscal)	Corporate Franchise Tax Exemption Development Loans
	
	Targeting of:
	  Pension Funds
	  Public Facilities
	  Procurement
	  Enterprise Zones
		IDA operations IRB usage local property tax exemption

(Regulatory)	Regulatory Relief Ombudsman Services Reserve Requirements (banking) Redlining (insurance) Enterprise Zones	Zoning
State-Local (Services)	Tourism Economic base and marketing data Enterprise Zones	Roads, Water, Sewer Site/Economic Base Data Small Business Seminars Business Incubators
Federal (Fiscal)	SBA 503 loans (to local development corporations) CDBG small cities grants UDAGs EDA Grants CDBG entitlements	Local Development Corporation (loans from own sources, state or CDBG/UDAG)

Table 3.1 sets out the major economic development tools often available to local governments and shows which of these are authorized by the state or federal governments. The table indicates which of these are *permissive* (state enabling legislation and local implementation) and which are *constrained* (state or federal decision required for the program to be used).

Local Development Corporations

Local autonomy is enhanced by the interaction between local development corporations and multiple program funding sources. The Local Development

Corporation (LDC) is an extremely flexible development tool that is in operation at many locations around the country. It can be a for-profit or non-profit form and can engage in a number of useful development activities, including land assembly, direct financing, loan packaging, industrial park development, building rehabilitation, and the provision of business advisory services (Patterson 1967). LDCs have also become active in contracting with local governments to manage loan pools or area promotion activities.

In New York LDCs can draw on four types of funds for business investment:

Federal

SBA 503 loans (to the LDC for reloan)

State

Job Development Authority (JDA) Loans funded with general obligation bonds (LDC involvement required by the state for a firm to receive this loan)

Local

Communities can contract with LDCs to manage loan pools funded from Community Development Block Grant (CDBG) monies or Urban Development Action Grant (UDAG) loan repayments

Subscriptions or stock sales by the LDC

In addition to using these monies that are channeled through the LDC itself, many developers become involved in loan packaging, which includes commercial bank loans, SBA (Small Business Administration) guaranteed and SBA direct loans. Together these programs give developers in New York some flexibility in assembling below-market-rate financing for small firms. Major drawbacks to these funds (except for the local funds listed above) are that they are tied to the creditworthiness of the borrower and entail interest and principal repayments that begin soon after the loan is arranged. There is little to distinguish them from standard bank loans which accept only low levels of risk. In short, while these funds are available, they are difficult to turn toward entrepreneurial uses.

Exceptions are the funds coming from Community Development Block Grant (CDBG) and Urban Development Action Grant (UDAG) monies and from local subscriptions. Federal CDBG/UDAG funds have been used to capitalize revolving loan funds in many locations around the country. In some cases the fund is managed by the LDC under contract to the city and in others it is managed by the city itself. Smaller, younger firms have benefited a great deal from revolving funds. Local governments consider such funds attractive because they give a community some control over the economic changes taking place in it. Though scarce, these funds offer opportunities for entrepreneurial action. They will be discussed more fully in Chapter 6. Local subscriptions are usually a small portion of the financing picture, more often being allocated to operating expenses of the LDC. Corporation reserves are often used in bridge financing, however, when loan packages are being arranged and thus serve to increase the flexibility of local developers.

Industrial Development Authorities

Another important source of loan funds are Industrial Development Authorities (IDAs). In New York State, Industrial Development Authorities are established by special legislation as public benefit corporations organized under Article 18-A of the General Municipal Law. The device has been popular; 151 authorities were established between 1969 and 1981, although only about one-half of these actually issued bonds (New York State 1981). The authorities are empowered to acquire and dispose of personal property, acquire and alter or improve real property (land, buildings, equipment), make contracts and leases, and sell tax-exempt revenue bonds for certain purposes. IDAs are attractive to legislators in all states because they permit local governments to bypass state debt limits and constitutional restrictions on loans to private enterprises (Gray and Spina 1980).

Tax Exempt Development Bonds. The financing device used by IDAs is the Industrial Revenue Bond (IRB) which is treated by the Internal Revenue Service as a government bond exempting the purchaser from federal income tax. This gives them a lower interest rate than standard commercial loans. In New York, the bonds can be used for land, buildings, or equipment associated with manufacturing, warehousing, research, commercial, or industrial purposes. Until federal legislation changed in 1984, permissible projects included industrial pollution control facilities and winter recreation facilities (New York General Municipal Law Section 854). For many years, following their authorization in 1969, IDAs in New York were subject to very little state supervision. No state agency had to approve their bonding decisions and they were not required to be audited or to file reports on their loan disbursements. Authorities were not required to check into the credit of the firms or individuals assisted with IRBs (New York State 1974). A provision in Article 18-A that bond monies not be used to help firms moving from another location in the state has had little effect. In most cases IDAs make little distinction between in-state and out-of-state firms when deciding on eligibility (New York State 1981). The absence of state scrutiny gave IDAs some freedom to decide which firms they want to help. Most importantly there is no size requirement placed on the firm, in terms of sales, employees, or the number of jobs created. How IRBs were used indicated what priorities local developers had.

The relative freedom localities enjoyed in using IRBs up through the period covered by this research, ended with tax reform legislation in 1984. One important outcome was that the amount of tax exempt bonds that could be issued by states was limited for the first time, which reduced the availability of IRBs. The Tax Reform Act of 1986 further tightened the limits on the amount of bonds that can be issued. In 1987, states are permitted $75 per capita or $250 million, whichever is greater. In 1988 these limits decline to $50 per capita or $150 million. Bonds sold for primarily private use[1] can no longer be used for privately owned pollution control facilities, sports, convention or trade show facilities, industrial parks, or several other types of business activities ("Major Provisions" 1986, 2354). Banks, which have been heavy purchasers of IRBs, no longer are permitted to take the interest tax-free. Other restrictions were imposed as well (Porter 1986, 4–5). With the federal government restricting the use of IRBs, states with large IRB programs are in turn tightening their approval and targeting procedures ("Pennsylvania's Decline" 1986, 7–8).

Taxable Development Bonds. Increased restrictions on tax-exempt bonds have created interest in taxable bonds for economic development purposes. Developers have found that structuring a financial package with taxable bonds gives them more flexibility than they ever had with tax-exempt bonds. The taxable bond market is more challenging, however, which is forcing development authorities to be more sophisticated in analyzing deals and selling the bonds. In addition, developers will find it harder to offer low interest rates to the borrower or market issues smaller than $30 million. For small firms this may be a blessing in disguise since states, such as Massachusetts, are reserving their tax-exempt industrial development bond (IDB) allocations to firms with sales of under $30 million ("Conference Report" 1986, 4–7). While this is still much larger than what most people would consider a small firm, there is a chance that the average size of firms using tax-exempt bonds will decrease.

Market Constraints. Beyond the restrictions now in place on the tax-exempt financing mechanism, IDAs are also constrained by market forces. Their ability to sell bonds depends on the creditworthiness of the recipient firm that must pay off the bond. Their value in helping small, new firms is therefore limited in the same way bank loans are limited, i.e., unless the firm has a track record, it is hard to sell the bonds for it. IRBs and thus IDAs have the additional constraint of high transaction costs for bond counsel fees. Bonds for less than $400,000 are not cost effective for the lessee because closing costs wipe out any interest savings. Still, there are differences in the average size of loans given out by different IDAs. Among four counties examined in New York for this study, IDAs in Orange and Niagara counties sold only 9 to 10 percent of their bonds in amounts smaller than $350,000 between 1969 and 1981 while in Oneida and Dutchess 18 and 30 percent, respectively, of the bonds sold were below this figure. What this indicates is that IDAs in the latter two counties were pushing the lower limits of the IRB device and probably were helping smaller firms than IDAs in the first two counties.[2] As states move toward pooling of taxable bonds (not permitted under laws regulating tax-exempts) smaller firms will further benefit from access to bond markets that were formerly closed to them because of their small size ("Conference Report" 1986, 6).

Federal Funds: UDAG and CDBG

Community Development Block Grants. Federal Urban Development Action Grants (UDAGs) and Community Development Block Grants (CDBGs) inject a good amount of flexibility into local development finance for qualifying municipalities.[3] The Housing and Community Development Act of 1977 added economic development as one of the specific objectives of the Community Development Block Grant program. A number of options are open to cities in their use of CDBG funds. They can continue to do certain planning and land assembly activities that they have done in the past, and they can also undertake new economic development activities. Specifically, the 1977 act permitted two new activities:

the funding of (1) activities which are carried out by public or private nonprofit entities and are appropriate to meeting the needs and objectives of a grantee's community development plan, including purchase of real property, development of public facilities, and development of commercial and industrial facilities; and (2) activities undertaken by neighborhood-based nonprofit organizations, local development corporations or Small Business Investment Companies to carry out a neighborhood or community economic development project. (HUD 1980, X–2)

Governments were no longer limited to building parking garages or streets in support of business investment but could build new or redevelop existing buildings for industrial or commercial purposes or fund the advising and advertising activities of local development corporations. Prior to 1981, communities could not transfer Community Development monies directly to private for-profit entities although funds could be used for loans to private firms if they went through non-profit organizations first. This restriction prevented some cities from doing as much for business as they wanted. After the restriction was lifted, the city of Rome, New York, quickly moved to pledge $100,000 a year for three years to a revolving loan fund to be managed by Rome's LDC.

Urban Development Action Grants. Even before 1981, some federal funds were available for direct public leveraging through the UDAG program. Urban Development Action Grants were authorized by Title l of the Housing and Community Development Act of 1977. The UDAG is a project-specific capital grant available to public or private businesses in large cities in Standard Metropolitan Statistical Areas (SMSAs), small cities below 50,000 in population outside SMSAs and urban counties (having at least 200,000 in population and one city over 25,000 in population). UDAGs are targeted at locations with declining tax bases, population outmigration or stagnation, aged housing stock, and job lag or decline. Eligible uses for UDAGs include the purchase of land and equipment, constructing or rehabilitating buildings, and other uses related to the creation of jobs for low-income residents and opportunities for development (HUD n.d.; Freiser 1982). An important feature of UDAGs for entrepreneurial governments is that once a developer and the city win a UDAG, the repayments on the government's share of the investment are returned to the local government, not the federal government. In Utica, New York, UDAG repayments were allocated to a revolving loan program for economic development as early as 1978. Details on these programs are discussed in Chapter 6. Governments that take full advantage of these programs early on to develop locally controlled, equity-like funding tools are considered to be more enterprising than governments not using funding in this way.[4]

The value of CDBG and UDAG funds has diminished due to budget restrictions placed on these and other economic development financing tools at the federal level since 1981. Although the share of CDBG funds going to economic development has increased since 1981 (Herzik and Pelissero 1986) the total CDBG program has declined in constant dollars, making for stronger competition between economic development and other objectives of the program, such as revitalizing residential neighborhoods (Dommel 1984).

Tax Abatements

Every state allows local governments to abate property taxes for some portion of selected industrial and business investments for a period of years (Gray and Spina 1980). In New York, Section 485 of the Real Property Tax Law of New York State permits local governments to exempt from taxes for up to ten years real property that has undergone capital improvements consisting of construction, reconstruction, or improvement of depreciable property. At least five permanent jobs must be created for this benefit to apply. The amount of tax exemption can be any amount the locality chooses, up to 100 percent. Section 485B of the Tax Law is an automatic exemption that is given to firms making investments or improvements to property for commercial, business, or industrial activity. The exemption is for ten years, beginning at 50 percent and declining 5 percent each year. Local governments can decide not to grant any exemptions, however, or they can alter the level of exemption granted for different purposes.

Deciding what facility is eligible is up to the local tax assessor although a form providing information about the exemption must be filed with the state board of equalization and assessment. With these two provisions a local government could offer no property tax exemptions at all or up to 100% exemption for ten years if it desired. The provisions of these laws have proven more popular with cities and townships than with school districts.

SUMMARY: LOCAL GOVERNMENT AUTONOMY

Local governments enjoy a measure of discretion in designing policies to promote local small business. Their traditional development tools are changing; however, this may not be harmful to small business since they were never of much use to the small, new firm anyway.

There is no question that the job of the economic developer has become increasingly challenging in the 1980s. The traditional financing tools are disappearing and it is not yet clear what will take their place. There is more interest in helping the small firm but the government-sponsored financing tools continue to be rather inappropriate to the task. Because of these changes, community-based innovations in promoting development are springing up all across the country. For the proponent of small business, this is an opportunity to do more for small firms than seemed possible in the past when industrial recruitment was the primary method of economic development. The issue for a study of the impact of state and local policy on small business activity is not whether local governments are able to help such firms, but whether they have the desire to do so.

Because there are no state mandates on economic development policies, the level of development effort varies not only across states but also within states. Inadequacies in personnel or government structure or a lack of support among local businessmen and public officials mean that some locations have failed to use even the available tools very effectively. In contrast aggressive development managers can put together a program that does offer meaningful assistance to small firms. To do this they may have to adapt existing programs to local needs or draw in private sector resources for small business development (Council for Northeast Economic Action 1980). These are in fact entrepreneurial actions because they step outside established constraints and usual government roles.

If policy makers become serious about helping entrepreneurs it will be necessary to relax some of the traditional limitations on community discretion. Local leaders will also have to become more informed about how their community's structures and social networks contribute to or inhibit the production of entrepreneurial ideas and projects. It will no longer be possible to relegate economic development policy to a professional whose skills in marketing and loan packaging are all that is needed to bring about business investment. What will be needed is a focus on community development rather than economic development. While this gives community groups a greater scope for participation in defining what kind of economic future is desired for the community, it is much more challenging to guide such a diverse and wide-open process. In fact there is a real question about whether it can be "managed" at all.

In testing the impact of the entrepreneurial model we must recognize that local resources and government structures do have limits. Only by examining the effects of local policies in a variety of settings can we tell how these limits condition the impact of economic development policy on entrepreneurial activity. We will take up this empirical question in the next two chapters.

NOTES

1. Defined as bonds in which more than 10 percent of the funds raised are used for other than public purposes. Formerly the percentage allowed was 25 percent (Major provisions of the Tax Reform Act of 1986. Congressional Quarterly, October 4, 1986: 2354).

2. Bond size can be misleading since in Dutchess several of the bonds went to franchisees such as McDonald's for which the corporate parent provided backing.

3. If a city is over 50,000 in population or a county is over 200,000 (excluding cities receiving funds individually), they are automatically entitled to CDBG funds in the form of an annual grant. A smaller city can qualify for a grant by applying for a small cities' grant on a project basis. These cities must compete with other cities across the country for funding.

4. An important restriction on these programs before 1981 was that a grantee's community development program as a whole principally benefit low- or moderate-income persons and in addition *each* funded activity either principally benefit low- and moderate-income families or help prevent or eliminate slums or blight or meet other urgent community development needs (HUD 1980, X–2). In the depressed cities examined here this turned out to be no problem. After 1981 the only requirement was that any jobs created be available to such persons. At the same time it became possible for profit-making corporations to receive community development funds and, also, more economic development projects became eligible. As a result more cities channeled money into economic development between 1982 and 1983 (Dommel 1982).

Chapter 4

Measuring the Effects of Policy on Small Business Startups

Evaluating the effect of public actions on society is no easy task. The ideal measurement setting is where the policy is cleanly delivered to a group of select recipients who can be compared to another group not receiving the service. This research is designed to measure policy effects by comparing what happens in localities that have adopted entrepreneurial development policies to others that have not. The challenge is to eliminate as many other explanations of the variations in business births as possible while setting up a clean test of policy. This chapter describes how this was done.

POLICY AND BUSINESS STARTUPS: PREVIOUS STUDIES

The impact of public policies on small business startups has received virtually no rigorous empirical attention although a few statistical studies have been published. All explain the levels of business starts by using a variety of economic and policy variables, and two (Carlton and Pennings) use the same data set to measure business starts.[1]

Carlton's study used several indicators for tax and incentives policies: (1) average corporate tax rates for the two time periods studied; (2) average personal income tax rates for the same periods; (3) estimated effective property tax rates for the years 1967 and 1971; and (4) an index describing the presence or absence of fifteen state development incentives (Carlton 1979). Regarding the index, Carlton notes,

It would of course be an improvement if the index took into account the degree to which each incentive is actually used. Lack of data prevented the construction of such an index. Moreover, the decision on which fifteen policies to look at and the decision to weigh each policy equally are both arbitrary. We therefore do not have great confidence in this variable. (1979, 29)

Carlton found that neither the incentives index nor tax rates were related to birth levels. But regarding taxes he notes, "The data do not allow us to rule out the possibility that taxes *could* exert a strong negative effect on new locational activity" (1979, 15–16). The variables that Carlton did find significant were: wages, energy costs (for plastics and electronic components industries), amount of existing activity an industry had in the area, and the number of university graduates in appropriate disciplines.

Carlton's study is a sophisticated effort at modeling births econometrically. However, his operationalization of the policy variables fails to capture much of the variation in development policies. With better data his econometric approach is extremely powerful, but without adequate data to describe policy change, other better-specified variables accounted for more of the variation in birth rates.

Pennings (1982b) operationalized political climate in a completely different way. Pennings used factor scores to rank SMSAs on their "political quality of life." The scale scores were generated by a factor analysis of budgetary and social variables from 1972 (Ben-Chieh 1975). SMSAs were considered to have a higher quality of political life if they scored highly on five categories of indicators.[2]

Pennings found that SMSAs scoring well on political quality of life had fewer births than locations with lower scores. He had assumed that "a sophisticated, politically mature and well-informed citizenry would form an ideal environment for entrepreneurs." His ad hoc explanation for his finding was that politically healthy urban areas are better integrated and more cohesive, which might make it more difficult for deviant entrepreneurs to get support for their ideas. Also SMSAs ranked highly when they spent more of their funds on welfare, which may indicate they were also decaying. Higher-ranked SMSAs also paid their civil servants more, which could drive up wages. He concluded,

Politically healthy SMSAs are not ideal location areas for entrepreneurs. Rather, entrepreneurs tend to be active in those areas where political participation is low, local government is light, public welfare is less, and civil servants are not numerous and are less well paid. (1982b, 73)

Pennings calls the results enigmatic but they make sense if considered in light of the interregional changes in population and income occurring in the country over the last thirty years (Greenwood 1981; ACIR 1981b; 1980). Pennings's quality of life indicators were measured at one time—1970—and his analysis actually measures differences between SMSAs, not within individual SMSAs over time. His approach to measurement cannot show whether these variables were causally related to births or only correlates of whatever processes have made Southern and Western SMSAs grow more rapidly than those in the Midwest and Northeast. Pennings's analysis thus cannot identify the independent effect of policy when changes in energy availability and migration are taken out of the analysis. Since broader economic forces overwhelm policy variables it is important to control for them in some way.

Dennis (1986) used demographic, social, economic, and policy variables to explain the variation in two measures of business startup activity in fifty states in 1976–1978. The business start variables were the ratio of new independent firm starts to the number of existing independent firms and the ratio of starts per 1,000 population of the state (1986, 316–17). The public policy variables included measures of the state's tax effort,[3] governmental revenues per capita, and government employment. None of the policy variables were significant in explaining either indicator of business startups. The most significant indicators proved to be measures of population mobility, urbanization, and percentage of the population foreign born or first generation.[4] In contrast to theories of entrepreneurship regarding immigrant status as having a positive effect on startups, Dennis found the relationship to be negative in his data. Interestingly, variables sometimes mentioned as being important to startup activity, including percentage of science Ph.D.s, personal income or income growth, banking, and size of the business population proved not to be significant in explaining the variation in startup activity.

Like Carlton, the indicators Dennis used for public policy fail to adequately describe the range of policy initiatives governments are trying. Even if we had found that governmental revenues per capita were significant, for example, we could not tell what aspect of government fiscal activity was helpful to the entrepreneurial process. Also, being cross-sectional, the study cannot capture policy change over time in a unit of analysis. It is impossible to say that communities that adopted policies to promote entrepreneurship would actually see an increase in startup rates.

THE DESIGN OF THIS STUDY

The design for this study is in the form of a natural experiment: patterns of small-firm startups will be examined across locations that have undertaken different levels of policy entrepreneurship. Statistical controls alone could not be used because it would have been difficult to collect policy information across a large enough number of sites. Even if the policy information could be gathered, the available time series data on business startups was too short to use time series analytic techniques. Yet it is important to look at how startups change over time if we want to determine whether or not policy is important. These considerations led to the selection of a type of quasi-experimental design, the control series design, as a way to improve upon previous studies. This design relies on the work of Cook and Campbell on quasi-experimental research designs (see Appendix A).

Selecting Locations to Study Impact of Entrepreneurial Policies

Four New York State counties form the basis for the empirical test of the entrepreneurial model. Two counties that followed active entrepreneurial policies are contrasted to two economically and demographically similar counties that adopted fewer policies beneficial to small, new firms. These will be called entrepreneurial and non-entrepreneurial sites. Efforts were made to select counties that showed either very high or very low levels of policy entrepreneurship. Because of the small N and qualitative nature of the policy data, only in sites where the policy efforts differed greatly is policy likely to have a detectable impact on business behavior.

In addition to the four "case study counties," data on business activity was assembled for eleven other counties in the states of Ohio, Michigan, and Pennsylvania. Data from these counties are used to establish baseline figures for business birthrates. Five of these counties were used as the baseline for the distressed counties, the other six for the healthy counties. These "baseline counties" thus furnish data with which to evaluate national business cycles as an explanation of fluctuations in birthrates.

In the text to follow, major issues in applying the comparative cases approach are discussed. These are: addressing internal threats to validity, selecting cases displaying different levels of policy entrepreneurship, and developing the framework of characteristics on which comparisons will be made.

The variables that must be held constant are economic conditions that are likely to affect business birthrates in different locations. Pennings (1982a) identified several local characteristics that had statistically significant impacts on business births in three manufacturing industries.[5] The characteristics were: size of the human population, population change, diversity of the organizational population across Standard Industrial Classifications (SICs), industry size, capital availability, and bank concentration. Baseline counties were selected on the basis of their similarities on four variables: population size in 1980, employment growth 1970–1980, population change 1970–1980, and industry differentiation in 1977.[6]

Nine counties in New York State fit these constraints. See Table 4.1. The counties, divided into those gaining and losing population, fall into two geographic groups. Four counties located along the Hudson north of New York City have benefited from the population dispersal taking place there. The other five are upstate counties that experienced declines in population and employment in the 1970s (Morrison 1978).

Distinguishing Levels of Policy Entrepreneurship

Selecting four case study counties from these nine involved several considerations: how policy entrepreneurship was defined; the need to make

Table 4.1
Potential Case Study Sites

County	1977 Diff Index	Avg Emp Chng(Pct)*		1980 Pop 000s	Pop* Change 70-80
		70-75	75-80		
Growing					
Dutchess	.51	1.8	1.3	245	10.2
Ulster	.67	(0.6)	4.2	158	12.0
Rockland	.69	3.1	3.9	260	12.9
Orange	.76	0.8	3.9	260	17.1
Distressed					
Niagara	.54	(3.5)	3.9	227	(3.5)
Broome	.59	(1.2)	2.7	214	(3.7)
Chautauqua	.62	**	1.8	147	(0.3)
Rensselaer	.63	(0.8)	1.5	152	(0.3)
Oneida	.70	(2.2)	2.5	253	(7.2)

* Figures in parentheses indicate declines.

** Less than 0.1 percent.

precise intercase comparisons of data; and the need to eliminate alternative explanations for observed levels of business birthrates in each location.[7]

The core meaning of policy entrepreneurship is to be found in what governments do about four issues that are susceptible to policy manipulation and that may enter into the small-business startup and location decision: capital, information, managerial ability, and political climate. To determine how aggressive a county had been in assisting small firms, an ideal type model was constructed from an array of policies that writers have identified as being helpful to small new firms. Included were actions that governments could take under presently available legislation. Policies fitting this constraint are set out in Table 4.2. Of prime concern in selecting policies was the question, is government sensitive to the needs of smaller firms and is it providing real, useful assistance that is more than boosterism? Most of the entries are self-explanatory but a few comments regarding matters of judgment need to be made about some of them.

True equity funds are available in only a few highly selective state programs. The more relaxed definition "equity-like" was used in classifying localities. A loan may become similar to equity under several conditions. One is subordination to other debt. SBA monies commonly require second position but some local funds accept a third position which will leave the government little after other creditors are satisfied. Another feature that makes funds equity-like is that payments on the interest or principal may be deferred for months or years. In some cases the flexibility attached to

Table 4.2
Operational Definition of Policy Entrepreneurship

Policy Innovativeness
        Availability of equity or equity-like funds
        Efforts to assemble public or private
          equity funds locally
        Willingness of local developers to risk
          resources on small or new firms
        Creation of incubator facilities for
          new or young firms
        Availability of technical assistance

Small Business Targeting
        Presence of an explicit small business
          component in local development services
        Amount of staff resources devoted to
          small firm concerns
        Percentage of capital funds channeled
          through development organizations into
          young ventures less than three years old
        Percentage of funds going to firms with less
          than twenty employees

Governmental Commitment
        Support of local governmental bodies for
          economic development
            -public monies channeled into loan programs
            -public monies aiding development bodies
        Characteristics of public support
            -level of funding
            -stability and trends in public monies
            spent on development matters
            -year in which programs first used locally
        Cooperation between county and municipal
          officials and economic developers on
          development matters

local loan pools is shown when governments delay collecting from firms in trouble. Such actions can turn loans into something resembling true equity. The primary criterion is that regular principal and interest payments are reduced or delayed.

Providing technical assistance is placed under *Policy Innovativeness* because few development organizations offer such assistance despite the fact that small businesses are often found to have management weaknesses. Technical assistance is determined by the needs of the firm but in general may be directed at concerns facing management: accounting, finance, marketing, labor relations, space management, resource management, and negotiating contracts or marketing arrangements. The development agency may not provide all these aids itself but could help the firm decide whether professional assistance was needed and where to find it. Serving as an information clearinghouse was considered to be supplying technical assistance.

Small Business Targeting is in a separate category to emphasize that unless small firms receive explicit attention, aid is likely to gravitate toward larger, established firms. It was not enough to say that "our assistance is available to all local firms" or that "most of our assistance goes to smaller firms." Organizations had to set a high priority on assisting small, new firms by setting aside staff and material resources for them.

Judgments about how much an area's development activity benefited small firms relied heavily on information about the size and age of firms receiving financial assistance. Loan records of commonly available programs (IRBs, SBA, JDA, RLFs) were examined to determine the proportion of aid going to small, new firms. Financing received the most attention because access to capital is the biggest constraint on the survival of small firms. Getting money to such firms is perhaps the most difficult thing government can be expected to do.

The entries under *Governmental Commitment* bring attention to the fact that a government's "attitude" toward business is conveyed by the financial support and political capital politicians devote to economic development. It is common for governments to advertise that they are a friend of business when all they offer is a friendly handshake. One indicator of the priority placed on economic development was the level and stability of financial support governing bodies gave to development agencies and activities. Another was the ability of political leaders and business interests to sustain interest in projects designed to improve the economy.

Judging how entrepreneurial a particular site was rested on four considerations: (1) what kind of policies were adopted by the sites, (2) how innovative they were, (3) how interested developers and politicians seemed to be in small, new firms and how knowledgeable they were about their needs, and (4) how commited to substantive economic development the governments seemed to be. Interviews and archival research were used to determine whether any level of government carried out the activity, when it was started, how strongly the effort was being supported locally, and how local development policy changed between 1975 and 1982.

Identifying Research Sites: Case Study Counties

Using information from a telephone survey of local development professionals,[8] the counties were identified as to the level of effort in promoting small firms. Policy effort is a judgmental ranking based on the number of different initiatives locations had adopted, and the amount of financial and manpower resources committed to newer firms and methods versus traditional policies and business targets. Niagara and Dutchess counties were not very energetic on small-business issues during the study period, while the other counties were. In studying policy effects, it is important to compare counties with similar levels of economic health. Although population loss does not necessarily result in stagnation (Morrison 1978), it is often associated with stagnant or declining economic conditions. The four counties selected for close study were Niagara, Oneida, Dutchess, and Orange. Ulster and Rensselaer were dropped because their populations were on the low end of my desired range (150,000–260,000). Broome was dropped because while it and Oneida were equally innovative, Oneida was a more accessible research site.

Choosing Baseline Counties

What are here called baseline counties are used to address a threat to the validity of this research, the national business cycle. What follows is a description of how this was handled.

Data on economic and demographic characteristics were collected for nine counties in New York and thirty-two counties in the states of New Jersey, Pennsylvania, Illinois, Indiana, Ohio, and Michigan. One type of economic data was employment by thirty-two two-digit SIC categories for the forty-one counties. Other variables were chosen to highlight industrial similarities and differences in wealth, economic growth, and population changes. Variables used were the following:

Average Employment Growth 1970–1975 (recessions prominent)

Average Employment Growth 1976–1980 (expansion prominent)

Median Family Income 1980

Population Change 1970–1980

Dummy variable indicating if the county is a suburb of a large city

1980 Population

Average Unemployment Rate for the years 1977, 1978, and 1980

Employment across 32 two-digit SIC divisions

These variables were used in SAS's cluster procedure (SAS 1982) to find the counties that were most similar to the case study counties. The cluster map of counties based on these variables is presented in Appendix D.

The case study counties and the baseline counties that clustered most closely with them are presented in Table 4.3. Data from growing and distressed baseline counties will be used in reference to case study counties in the same group. Discussion of these comparisons is presented in Chapter 5.

Table 4.3
Case Study and Baseline Counties

Case Study Counties	Baseline Counties
Growing Counties	
New York	
Orange	Washtenaw, MI
Dutchess	Beaver, PA
	Lorrain, OH
	Lake, OH
	Butler, OH
	Trumbull, OH
Distressed Counties	
Oneida	Kalamazoo, MI
Niagara	Saginaw, MI
	Lackawanna, PA
	Northampton, PA
	Broome, NY

METHODOLOGICAL SUMMARY

Quasi-experimentation is useful where more elegant methods are ruled out by the research setting, quality of available data, or the nature of the research hypothesis. These characteristics make it difficult to set up clear-cut tests of research hypothesis. Unfortunately, all of these conditions apply in the present case and make ruling out rival hypotheses laborious and somewhat unsatisfactory.

In this chapter efforts to deal with these intransigent issues in selecting research sites have been discussed. The principal products are four case study counties, that are comparable in several important respects but differ on policy efforts, and a number of baseline counties that resemble their corresponding case study counties. How policy variables and business startups behave in these selected counties constitutes the test of the entrepreneurial model. The details of this test are taken up in Chapters 5 and 6.

Notes

1. Two of the studies (Carlton and Pennings) used the same data set to measure firm births: a sample of data from the Dun and Bradstreet records for between twenty-eight and forty-two SMSAs for two periods, 1969–1971 and 1972–1975. The data cover three high-growth manufacturing industries: Fabricated Plastic Products (SIC 3079); Communication Transmitting Equipment (SIC 3662); and Electronic Components (SIC 3699). The data show the number of new businesses started in

each industry for the years 1969–1976. The third (Dennis) used a U.S. Small Business Administration data set constructed using Dun and Bradstreet records.

2. Indicators were organized into the following categories: Informed Citizenry (e.g., Sunday newspaper circulation and number of radio stations per 1,000 population); Percent of eligible population casting a vote in the previous presidential election; Professionalism (e.g., average monthly salary for public employees, municipal employment per 1,000 population, police protection per 1,000 population); Performance (e.g., violent crime rates, local government revenue per capita, indexes for community health and education); Welfare Assistance (e.g., per capita local expenditures on public welfare, average monthly Aid to Families with Dependent Children [AFDC] benefits).

3. Tax effort was measured by dividing revenue raised by the state's tax capacity.

4. Dennis examined the total number of business starts and the number for six one-digit industrial categories. His model produced R^2s between .68 and .80 in different industries.

5. Fabricated Plastic Products (SIC 3079), Communication Transmitting Equipment (SIC 3662), and Electronic Components (SIC 3699).

6. A discussion of these variables can be found in Mokry (1985).

7. A common criticism of the case study approach is that the data collected tends to be highly particularistic, making it difficult to compare cases or generate and test hypotheses (Miles 1979, Yin 1981). Rigorous analysis is possible, however, if several conditions are met.

1. A parsimonious theoretical framework is developed that focuses attention on essential "topics" (Yin, 1981) or "key variables" (Lijphart, 1971, 690).

2. Systematic and reproducible methods are used to generate core data from each site (McClintock, Brannon, and Maynard-Moody 1979).

3. The data are collected in a way that allows plausible rival explanations of the phenomenon to be tested.

8. These definitions of policy entrepreneurship were used in both the initial and later stages of the research. To select case study counties a questionnaire was developed that asked local experts to provide information on how extensively a county and its municipalities had adopted the initiatives. The questionnaire is presented as Appendix C. Questions 2, 3, 4, and 9 cover policy innovativeness; 4, 7, and 8 small-business targeting; and 1, 5, and 6 policy commitment. Telephone interviews, averaging twenty to thirty minutes, were conducted with representatives of local development corporations, industrial development authorities, chambers of commerce, and departments of planning or economic development at the municipal and county level in seven of the nine potential counties. Rockland and Chautauqua were not canvassed because an acceptable array of research sites was assembled before they were reached.

Chapter 5

Development Policy in Four New York State Counties

Two of the case study counties, Dutchess and Orange, had large increases in population and employment in the 1970s. Niagara and Oneida, on the other hand, lost population and experienced low or sometimes negative employment change during the decade. While each county resembles its partner economically, an examination of the financing programs, technical or managerial assistance available, and the political climate of the sites indicates that the counties differ on their levels of policy effort and nature of the policies in use. Characteristics of the paired counties are such that the record of business births and survival in them presents a useful test of the model of entrepreneurial policy discussed in Chapter 2.

ECONOMIC CHANGES 1967–1977

Niagara and Oneida experienced similar economic changes between 1967 and 1977 centered on the loss of manufacturing employment. Dutchess and Orange both grew but the sources of growth were somewhat different. To gain perspective on the economic changes occurring in the counties, information will be presented on the level of employment, the growth of personal income, and changes in the sectoral makeup of area employment.

Employment Level

The level of employment for various years in the 1970s compared to the level in 1970 is set out in Figure 5.1. Several things should be noted. First, employment trends in the four counties are similar, peaks and valleys appear at approximately the same points. Second, all four counties start the decade slightly below their 1970 level but Dutchess and Orange soon enter on a

Figure 5.1
Employment Level in Study Counties 1971–80 (1970 base)

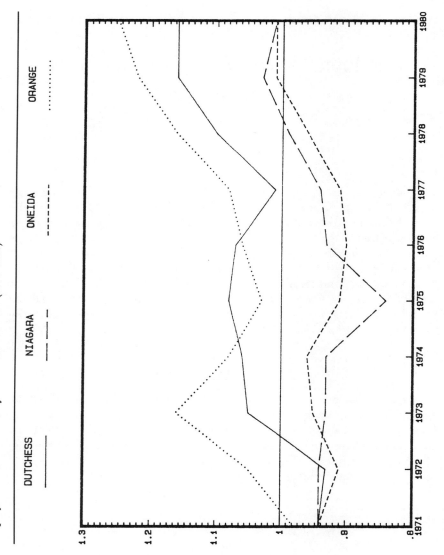

Note: 0.9 = 90% of 1970 level.   1.1 = 10% above 1970 level.

steady growth path while Niagara and Oneida remain below their 1970 employment level for most of the decade.[1]

While both Niagara and Oneida have increasing levels of employment after the 1975 recession, not until 1979 do either of them recover the number of jobs they had in 1970, and they continued to create jobs at a very low rate throughout the period.[2] Although employment levels in growing and distressed counties do not differ dramatically, each county operates at a level closer to the other member of its pair than to counties in the other pair. This is evidence that members in each pair respond similarly to national business cycles. This reduces the chance that business cycles explain fluctuations in business startup rates in these counties.

Personal Income

Changes in personal income also show that counties in a pair behave alike. Between 1970 and 1979 personal income increased 27.7 percent in Orange and 23.5 percent in Dutchess. At the same time, personal income in Oneida rose only 8.4 percent and in Niagara, 16.7 percent. (New York State Dept. of Commerce 1980; New York State, SUNY, Albany 1983).

Employment Change

The employment mix changed in similar ways within each pair as well. In Niagara and Oneida counties, deindustrialization was occurring at a rapid rate. Table 5.1 shows the aggregate number of jobs lost or gained in five industrial sectors. The loss of manufacturing jobs in Oneida and Niagara counties was hemorrhagic, over 10,000 manufacturing jobs disappeared from each county. Dutchess and Orange also lost manufacturing over the 1967–1977 period but their losses were not so severe. Moreover, manufacturing rebounded in the latter counties in the middle 1970s (data not shown in table). The number of manufacturing positions in Dutchess grew 4.4 percent between 1972 and 1977 and in Orange, 1.3 percent. Meanwhile Niagara and Oneida each lost 12 percent of their manufacturing jobs between 1972 and 1977 (U.S. Department of Commerce, Bureau of the Census *County Business Patterns* 1972 and 1977).

Growing and Declining Industries

These changes produced a different mix of employment in 1977 than existed in 1967. In Niagara, manufacturing declined from 64 percent of the work force in 1967 to 49 percent in 1977. For Oneida comparable figures are 45 percent and 33 percent, for Dutchess 50 percent and 43 percent, and in Orange 39 percent and 29 percent. The shifts in the sectoral distribution of jobs were not due to a declining manufacturing base alone. Service jobs

Table 5.1

Net Employment Change in Five Industrial Sectors in Case Study Counties
1967–1977

	Number (Percentage Change)			
	Dutchess	Orange	Niagara	Oneida
Manuf.	-845 (-0.03)	-1,648 (-9.7)	-12,273 (-27.6)	-10,211 (-33.4)
Whole.	-732 (-23.0)	944 (36.9)	566 (32.4)	94 (2.7)
Retail	3,431 (41.0)	3,354 (36.0)	2,235 (21.9)	1,198 (9.8)
FIRE*	314 (15.1)	751 (32.6)	290 (17.3)	844 (22.0)
Services	4,545 (47.2)	4,793 (66.4)	4,567 (62.4)	3,456 (31.7)

Source--County Business Patterns, 1967 and 1977

*FIRE--Finance, Insurance, Real Estate

expanded rapidly in all four counties (see Table 5.1). Niagara and Oneida
were helped quite a bit by the growth in service jobs. They created almost
as many jobs in FIRE and Services as did Dutchess and Orange Counties.
Without this rate of job creation, the economies of Niagara and Oneida
would be in much poorer shape than they are.

One final perspective on the nature of economic change taking place in
these counties is to examine in more detail which industries are growing or
declining. The figures cited below come from County Business Patterns (1967
and 1977).

Total employment in Dutchess County grew by 13 percent between 1967
and 1977, in large part because IBM (which is headquartered in the county
and employs directly and indirectly almost one-third of the work force) was
expanding at a rapid rate. After Medical Services (3,600 jobs), the largest
number of jobs were added in IBM strongholds: Non-electrical Machinery
and Electrical and Electronic components which together grew by over 4,000
jobs between 1967 and 1977. Seven industries added between 250 and 1,000
jobs, including Business and Educational Services, Communications, and
Retail Food Operations. Few industries lost large numbers of employees

although Electric, Gas, and Sanitation Services lost 1,750 jobs, Wholesaling 740, and Textiles 500.

Orange County's job growth occurred across a broad range of sectors that individually added moderate numbers of jobs, but together increased the county's employment by 19 percent between 1967 and 1977. The largest number of new jobs appeared in Medical Services (3,500) and Eating/Drinking Establishments (1,400). Between 500 and 1,000 jobs were added in Wholesaling, Banking, Chemicals, General Merchandise, and Food Retailers. Industries adding between 250 and 500 jobs were Printing, Primary Metals, Fabricated Metals, Transportation Equipment, and Business, Legal, and Educational Services. Orange County lost employment in Textiles (1,200), Leather Goods (680), and Electrical and Electronic Components, primarily television tubes (600). It is a matter of frustration to people in Orange that its electronics industry is practically nonexistent while just across the Hudson, in Dutchess County, computer and integrated circuits manufacturing flourishes.

Overall, Niagara's employment fell 6.3 percent between 1967 and 1977. Manufacturing jobs declined in most classifications but this sector also contributed the largest single collection of new jobs, over 5,000, in Non-Electrical Machinery (specifically Refrigeration and Service Machinery). Medical Services and Restaurants added 1,900 and 1,400 jobs, respectively. Service industries, such as Business (670) and Educational Services (800 jobs), also grew over the ten-year period. The list of declining sectors is heavily populated with manufacturing classifications, with which Niagara Falls has long been associated. Paper, Chemicals, Electrical Machinery, Transportation Equipment, Primary Metals, and Printing lost almost 17,000 jobs between 1967 and 1977. This large decline in manufacturing placed a great strain on the local economy that growing firms in manufacturing, retail, and services could not make up.

Oneida's experience was similar to Niagara's, its employment falling 9.3 percent between 1967 and 1977. Bright spots in the economy were Medical Services and Restaurants where approximately 5,000 jobs were added. Developers in the area are also very hopeful about several rapidly growing computer and peripherals manufacturing firms whose 1,600 new jobs appeared in the Non-Electrical Machinery category. Smaller numbers of jobs were added in Business Services, Insurance, and Communication where together 1,400 jobs were added. Declining industries in Oneida are similar to those in Niagara, led by Electrical Machinery and Chemicals which declined by about 5,700 jobs. Textiles, Paper, Primary Metals, and Air Transport together declined by 2,400 jobs. Deindustrialization in Oneida was less pronounced than in Niagara primarily because its economy had already lost many textiles, railroading, and metalworking firms before 1960 (Crisafulli 1960).

How Comparable Are the Study Sites?

Every locality has unique local experiences and trends that make it different from any other. Does the evidence indicate that the paired counties are similar enough to serve as case studies?

Niagara and Oneida are quite similar in their sources of economic stress and their trends in employment and personal income. Manufacturing is more dominant in Niagara than in Oneida but both see their economic future as lying outside manufacturing. When we consider their economies alone, neither site appears to be an especially promising location for startups. Population is stagnant and markets shrinking for consumer products. Given the history of employment change in the late 1960s to mid–1970s one would not expect sudden jumps in business startup rates due to natural economic change alone.

Dutchess and Orange are similar in their income and job creation trends. They are quite different in their sources of growth, however, Dutchess's being built on IBM and Orange's on a diverse array of small manufacturing, wholesaling, services, and retail firms. Despite their differences, however, both could serve as good locations for new businesses; both counties have the wealth and emerging opportunities that may spark the interest of entrepreneurs. For this reason we would expect that startup rates would be generally similar unless some other factor comes into play. The question at hand, of course, is whether policy differences do come into play.

LOCAL EFFORTS: RESOURCES, INFORMATION, AND POLITICAL CLIMATE

Development policies in each county can be understood by examining three environmental characteristics identified in Chapter 2: Resources, Information, and Political Climate. The counties in economic distress, Oneida and Niagara, will be discussed first and then the growing counties of Orange and Dutchess. Development organizations and resources available in these counties during the time studied are described in Appendix B.

Distressed Counties: Niagara and Oneida

Financing. Capital is the primary issue for new firms and, on this dimension, governments in Oneida County are much more entrepreneurial than those in Niagara County in the period 1975–1982. Oneida County has four revolving loan funds (RLFs), the oldest of which began operating in 1979. These supply low-interest subordinated debt for a wide variety of purposes, including new construction, rehabilitation, equipment, and working capital. The subordination and low interest (in some cases 0 percent but usually averaging 70 percent of the prime rate at time of closing) give small firms

Table 5.2
Number of Loans by Industry in Oneida and Niagara Counties

	OCIDC	NCIDA	RLFs
Manuf.	21	32	19
Whole.	4	3	1
Retail	6	0	33
Services	7	1	13
FIRE	8	2	11

OCIDC--Oneida County Industrial Development
      Corporation
NCIDA--Niagara County Industrial Development
      Agency
RLFs--Revolving Loan Funds
FIRE--Finance,Insurance, Real Estate

access to capital at extremely favorable rates and help to leverage bank financing by reducing the lender's exposure. In some cases interest payments have been deferred for up to three months and repayments rescheduled when firms have run into financial difficulties. All the RLFs require a mixture of personal funds and bank financing; they are limited to thirty to forty percent of project costs.

In contrast, the single RLF in Niagara County began operation in 1981 and its first financing was tied up in a large downtown shopping mall. A number of small retailers in the mall benefited from a unique arrangement between the city and the developer that required the developer to supply front-end working capital for small or first-time retailers to allow them to set up in the mall. Approximately $600,000 of the RLF's $1.2 million fund went to these equipment and working capital loans. The county's major funding program is the county IDA and its work has been mostly with firms having over 100 employees.

Table 5.2 sets out the percentage distribution of loans by source and by industry. NCIDA has placed few bonds outside manufacturing because its financing tool, the industrial revenue bond, is most appropriate for construction of new facilities or buying equipment. Although OCIDC figures include IRB loans, they also include SBA and JDA monies, which have a wider range of uses. The revolving loan funds show the most diverse funding pattern. The large number of retail loans reflects the urban redevelopment purposes of the source program (HUD's CDBG and UDAG programs). Because Niagara's IDA has placed so few loans outside manufacturing, later comparisons are based on this sector only.

The presence of RLFs in Oneida County results in more funding for younger, smaller firms than would otherwise be the case. Table 5.3 displays

Table 5.3
Revolving Loan Fund Activity in Oneida County: Manufacturing Loans

Firm Age	NCIDA	RLFs*
3 yrs or less	3	11
4 yrs or more	31	8

$$\text{Chi sq} = 15.2$$
$$p = <\ .001$$
$$\text{Phi sq} = .29$$

* Combined Activity of four Revolving Loan Funds (RLFs)

the number of manufacturing loans by firm age for NCIDA and the four revolving loans in Oneida County.

Revolving loan fund monies are significantly more likely to go to firms three years of age or younger than are those from the IDA. A similar, although more modest, difference is found if one compares Oneida RLFs to standard SBA or JDA loans or IRBs available through the Oneida County Industrial Development Corporation (OCIDC) (Chi sq = 7.04; Phi sq = .18). In other words a device such as an RLF is necessary if localities are to break out of the security-conscious loan decisions of banks or bank-like loan programs.[3] This finding is important because the only OCIDC activities included here are those in which it used funds arranged through the SBA, New York State Job Development Authority (JDA), and banks. These represent the standard debt sources that most small businessmen must turn to for financing; they are run conservatively and make loan security a high priority.[4]

Differences in the age of firms aided can be explained by the restrictions on the IRB and other standard debt instruments. These loan devices discriminate against young firms because firms must have a two-or three-year credit history. Also, IRBs offer borrowers no advantages if the bond is for less than $400,000 because transaction costs associated with bonding attorneys are fixed, regardless of the size of the bond. It is not surprising, then, that fewer young firms are able to use IRBs or other development loan programs.

Niagara and Oneida also differ in the size of firms receiving assistance, whether we consider RLF or standard-source loans in Oneida. Figures comparing NCIDA investments to the two sources in Oneida are set out in Table 5.4.

Table 5.4 shows that agencies in Oneida County provide more assistance to smaller firms than the Industrial Development Agency in Niagara has

Table 5.4
Manufacturing Loans by Size of Firm in Oneida and Niagara Counties

Number of Employees	NCIDA	RLF	NCIDA	OCIDC
20 or less	3	13	3	15
21 or more	31	6	31	7

	Chi sq = 18	Chi sq = 22.0
	p = <.001	p = <.001
	Phi sq = .36	Phi sq = .39

been able to do. This would provide more resources for young firms.[5] If financing is a consideration for small-business owners, the financing policies followed in Oneida could result in more startups.

A final indicator that RLF loans are assisting more risky firms is the loss rate. Banks look for a target loss rate on commercial loans (percentage of loan value that is not fully recovered) of less than 1 percent (Morris; McEnroe interviews). However, the combined loss rate for the RLFs through 1982 was approximately 10 percent. As the administrator of one program observed, they are very aware of their responsibility for soundly managing the public's funds but they also know that they cannot only invest in bankable deals if they are to have an impact on local conditions.

It might be argued that while these differences in loan patterns are statistically significant, they are of little practical consequence, since RLFs are so small relative to commercial loans or even other public funding sources. For the period in which RLFs were operating (1979–1982) NCIDA placed $107 million in industrial revenue bonds (IRBs) compared with only $2.78 million in investments for the RLFs. However, the actual dollar value of assistance is probably less important than the fact that the effort is being made to create and manage a development fund locally. One official, who was influential in getting city funds committed to Rome's RLF, made it clear that the effort was being made to make the community's economy more independent and flexible by having a publicly controlled source of funds that was not tied to bank interest rates or loan decisions made by bank officers. Rome is committed to putting more CDBG monies into their RLF (as is Utica), and so the funds will not only grow but their impact will be multiplied because the funds will revolve.[6] Not to be ignored is Schmenner's observation that the symbolism behind government's actions is as important as the policy's substantive effect on business costs. Putting dollars into an RLF of which a good portion goes to younger, smaller firms sends the message that local leaders are interested in and supportive of such firms.

In this regard it is significant that Oneida County made a one-time grant of $500,000 to the Oneida County Industrial Development Corporation that was used to capitalize a revolving loan fund operated by OCIDC. This money was appropriated from county tax revenues on top of the county's annual contribution of $125,000 to OCIDC's operating expenses. Actions such as this indicate that Oneida was highly supportive of business development after 1978.

Venture Capital. Neither site has successfully set up private or publicly funded venture financing, although every development professional questioned said venture financing was a major weakness of their areas. One developer in Oneida said venture capital programs had been "argued about" but nothing was set up. A partial substitute in Oneida County is the low-interest subordinated financing available through the RLFs, and the director of Mohawk Valley Economic Development District (MVEDD) stated that his agency instigated their RLF because it was clear that affordable financing for small or new firms was simply not available in upstate New York (Ladd interview).

Niagara officials recognized the need for venture capital but no fund has been organized either publicly or privately. In 1981 the county planning department, in response to a request from a legislator, undertook a detailed study of the venture capital issue and ways of supplying it locally. The study made a number of recommendations for action but nothing has been done. Further, unlike Oneida, only one RLF has been established as a partial substitute through low-interest subordinated loans (Niagara Falls' LDC) and it operates only within the boundaries of that city.

Facilities. Neither site developed incubators for new firms during 1975–1982. Both sites assist firms to find facilities but no special attention is given to small firms. Niagara County IDA and the Niagara Falls LDC were involved in a major downtown shopping mall that directly helped a number of new firms. The county also set aside $500,000 for an incubator facility that by mid–1984 still had not been constructed.

Information

All sources said that their staff were flexible—people were assigned to assist firms and troubleshoot as needed. There were no formal ombudsmen, but in one agency (OCIDC) an individual was designated as a small-business resource person, a position created in 1979 along with the IDC's Small Business Department. Responsibilities included organizing small-business seminars, maintaining a library of publications of interest to small firms, and helping in developing business plans and arranging financing. The agency has been consulted by up to 120 individuals or small firms annually. As many as thirty individuals a year are in what might be considered a startup situation. OCIDC bills itself as a "one stop shop" and it does appear that the staff could offer a range of useful advice to the new firm as well as the established small business. MVEDD has two staff assistants plus the director who provide advice about developing business plans and arranging bank financing.

Niagara County, in contrast, had no established technical assistance program to offer small firms over most of the 1975–1982 period. The Niagara Falls LDC works with small firms through its tourism and downtown revitalization efforts but has no staff working primarily with small or new firms. The director said the staff (one assistant) is simply too small to become involved in giving technical assistance on a regular basis (McCoy interview). The county Economic Development Department had no staff directed just at small business but did have a person responsible for tourism, an industry populated by small firms. The tasks were not geared toward management assistance but toward advertising and organizing annual events such as a fishing tournament. The IDA has a director and one staff person who are primarily oriented toward placing IRBs, and as was seen earlier these go predominantly toward firms over twenty employees in size. In short, in the 1975–1982 period the county had little to offer small, new firms in terms of staff time or technical assistance.[7] When staff did work with small firms it was as an adjunct to other duties.

Political Climate

Oneida County. The political climate of Oneida County provides an interesting contrast with that in Niagara. In the 1974–1978 period, describing political relations in Oneida as tumultuous and strained would be putting it mildly. In 1978, changes in political and administrative leadership brought a more coordinated use of financial and staff resources and a strengthening of formal and informal links between development agencies, political bodies, and the financial community. Niagara had no battle wounds to overcome, but neither did its development activities jell into more than intermittent cooperation on individual projects. Its efforts might be described as being in hibernation during this period.

Edward Hannah, mayor of Utica between 1974 and 1977, was a mercurial figure who feuded with the county executive, newspapers, banks, and the chamber of commerce during a good part of his first term. Development issues often became embroiled in controversy, including the search for a developer to put a hotel in downtown Utica, bus service to Utica's suburbs, and where to locate an upper division college of the SUNY system. Mayor Hannah abruptly cut off Utica's financial support for OCIDC in 1974 for what he termed its director's "cloak and dagger" methods in dealing with Miller Brewing Company after it passed over Oneida County for its new Northeastern brewery (*Utica Observer-Dispatch* 4/10/74). The county executive, William Bryant, in turn criticized Hannah's "loud, abusive, and hypocritical conduct. . . . which will not do anything for the Utica area" (4/11/74). At other times Hannah called the Utica Area Chamber of commerce a "country club" and "not worth the powder to blow it to hell" (5/22/74) and dubbed it the "Chamber of No Commerce" on a New York City radio show (8/26/74).

Divisions within the county went deeper than Hannah's personality, however. One observer familiar with events in that period commented that "everybody wanted to take the lead and the credit" for economic development. A great deal of mistrust prevailed between political bodies and reached into the development agencies as well; the heads of OCIDC and MVEDD "didn't speak to each other for three years" according to this source. Not only were coordinated efforts impossible to develop under these conditions but the different bodies undercut each other's efforts.

The elections of a new Utica mayor, Stephen Pawlinga, in 1977 and a new county executive, Sherwood Boehlert, in 1978 brought to office individuals who appeared to be serious about creating workable development tools. A number of the county's major programs benefiting small firms originated after 1978, including the RLF programs (Utica's—1978, MVEDD's—1979, Rome's—1981, the county's—1982) and OCIDC's small business department (1979). Also beneficial to small firms was the new effort by all four development agencies to provide "one stop" service on location, financing, and regulatory matters. One outcome is the single application being developed for all RLFs in the county. As early as 1980, different RLF monies were being pooled on specific projects.

Between 1978 and 1982 governments allocated significant amounts of money to economic development matters. Oneida County Industrial Development Corporation's revolving loan fund was funded by county tax dollars, and the Rome and Utica RLFs received their seed capital from Community Development Block Grant monies. Rome chose to contract with a local development corporation operated by the chamber of commerce to service its RLF, which helped remove fears of politically motivated loan decisions. There was also greater cooperation in specific projects; for example, a vacant knitting mill sitting on Utica's city line was rehabilitated into a large factory outlet mall in part because of support from both Utica and the county for elements of the project.

These developments did not signal an end to separatist tendencies; for example, Pawlinga created Utica's own IDA in 1981 despite criticism that it duplicated the county's IDA (Utica *Observer-Dispatch* 1/17/81). Yet cooperation and greater understanding were clearly evident.

Taken together these actions since 1978 present a significant contrast with the division and unfocused efforts prevailing in the county up to that time. If the term *political climate* has any meaning, it seems that entrepreneurs looking at the county in 1980 would see a very different picture than he or she would if the year 1974 were examined. If the willingness to work with business and supply some missing components does affect the startup decision, it seems reasonable to argue that the climate for entrepreneurship was much better by 1981 and 1982 in the county than in 1975 or 1976.

Niagara County. Niagara County government's commitment to development is characterized by success on major projects but also by a lack of a sustained working relationship between county agencies, the three cities, and their respective chambers of commerce. Most sources commented on the county's disorganized economic development apparatus. Up to 1979 county efforts on economic development were limited to providing one-half of the budget for IDA (approximately $18,000 per year between 1975 and 1977) and to carrying out economic research, planning, grant work, and tourism promotion by the county's Department of Planning and Economic Development. Between 1972, when the IDA was organized, and 1975, it lacked a full-time director, and when one was appointed he found he had to spend the first year and a half merely informing area firms of the IDA's existence and searching for projects in which IRBs were feasible. A policy statement he prepared for the IDA board in 1976 listed the priorities of the agency as being 1) retaining industry; 2) helping existing industry to expand; and 3) encouraging new industry to locate in the county. He observed that the IDA had nothing to offer smaller firms because IRBs are impractical for projects of less than $400,000 (Memo from Irving Clark to NCIDA Board, 3/12/76).

During this time the IDA acquired the reputation of being inaccessible to the smaller cities and towns in the county. Lockport, the county seat and home of the IDA, created its own IDA in 1981 because the mayor said the city had received virtually no IRB assistance. Other towns considered similar moves (*Niagara Falls Gazette* 3/7/81). In 1981 and 1982 the IDA under the spur of the county legislature began to establish stronger ties to the three major cities (Niagara Falls, Lockport, and North Tonawanda) (*Gazette* 3/14/81). One move was to put $30,000 into the chambers of commerce in each community for business promotion. Another, getting underway in 1983, expanded the IDA's board of directors from nine to twenty-two members to include more political and business representatives from county municipalities.

One ingredient that was and is still lacking at the county level in Niagara is a county executive or chief administrator. Legislative committees develop policy and oversee the departments carrying it out. Several informants pointed to the legislature's reluctance to relinquish some of its power to an enlarged and more autonomous IDA or county LDC as being a major handicap during the period under study. It was a major step for the county to authorize the IDA in the first place. Some legislators feared that a "monster" was being created, while others were concerned that the only control of legislature had over the agency was to appoint the board of directors (*Gazette* 4/19/72). As one source put it, the legislature "dabbles in economic development" but it does not understand development processes and lacks the time and inclination to find out what tools and organizations are needed locally. This began to change after 1980, but observers believed it was a major reason that the county had no strong organization to initiate projects and coordinate development within and between the cities. As John Orr, longtime chairman of the IDA's board, noted in 1980, there is a "crying need for coordination and consolidations of the county's economic development activities" (*Gazette* 3/30/80). Without a well-established development organization in the county, Niagara developed few programs to help small or new firms with any of the needs identified in the entrepreneurial model.

Most sources pointed to the cities as being better examples of governmental support for development efforts, especially Niagara Falls. Major initiatives in the city were the creation of the Economic Development Program in 1980, a Local Development Corporation in 1980 (accessing JDA, SBA, and private monies), and a $1.2 million Revolving Loan Program with UDAG seed money in 1981. Niagara Falls was also the first SBA 503 designee in the country and developed a rather innovative way to use HUD's Section 108 mortgage money (guaranteed by the Federal Financing Bank) as a development tool. As the director of the city's Economic Development Agency pointed out, however, neither program is designed for startup firms (McCoy interview). The Niagara Falls Local Development Corporation, along with NCIDA, participated in the downtown shopping mall and the incubator facility at the airport, both of which will provide opportunities for small business. While the city and county engaged in joint projects, such cooperation was infrequent and development expertise and contacts were not spread very widely across the county during the 1975–1982 period.

Growing Counties: Orange and Dutchess

Orange and Dutchess counties give little financial or technical assistance to young firms. Economic development in the 1975–1982 period was concerned almost exclusively with encouraging established firms to locate facilities in the area and with assisting established local firms to expand or upgrade their facilities.[8] Not until 1981 can any of the initiatives discussed in Chapter 2 under Innovativeness or Small Business Targeting be found in even one jurisdiction in either county.

Financing. The bulk of industrial or commercial financing available through development agencies in these counties consists of standard debt instruments: revenue bonds, New York State Job Development Authority low-interest loans, and SBA guaranteed loans. Orange and Dutchess were evenly matched in the amount of debt financing they made available to young firms between 1975 and 1980. Orange had two active Industrial Development Authorities, which together placed $38.8 million in bonds for twenty-one projects between 1970 and 1982. Of these, four (19 percent) went to firms three years old or younger and another four to firms that had fewer than twenty employees at the time. In addition to these two IDAs, various towns and cities established four others, one of which dissolved before placing any bonds, while the others placed only one bond each. This proliferation of marginal IDAs illustrates a dispersed approach to development promotion characteristic of Orange County.

Dutchess County had one active industrial development authority that began operations in 1980 and placed twenty bonds through 1982, five of which (25 percent) went to firms three years old or younger and nine (45 percent) to firms with less than twenty employees. Total IDA funding in the county between 1970 and 1982 amounted to $26.8 million dollars. The findings from IDAs in Dutchess, Orange, and Niagara counties are similar. None of the counties relying heavily on industrial revenue bonds has given as large a percentage of their financing assistance to young firms as RLFs have. Dutchess does seem to be trying to provide financing to small firms, however.

No revolving loan funds were active in Dutchess between 1975 and 1982, but in Orange County the City of Newburgh began an energetic development finance effort in 1981 that included RLFs. In 1980 Orange County was designated an urban county by the U.S. Department of Housing and Urban Development, making the cities of Newburgh and Middletown, as well as the county, eligible for commuity development block grant entitlement funds. (That is, these jurisdictions were automatically allocated a pool of CDBG funds each year.) With the infusion of this money, Newburgh initiated an aggressive economic development effort, devoting up to $650,000 per year of its $1.13 million CD entitlement to development activities. Between 1981 and 1983 approximately $700,000 of CD funds were used to finance expansions by local firms and provide assistance to firms moving into the city.[9] Another $200,000 was put into a revolving loan fund exclusively for minority ventures. The city also established an office responsible solely for economic development matters, the only one in the county. It administers the loan pools, helps prepare UDAG applications (eight have been won for local firms with less than fifty employees), and assembles financial packages by drawing on loan sources such as IRBs, JDA, and SBA.

The city is especially interested in small, growing firms. Speaking of the city's financing programs, the city's first director of the development agency commented,

We want to work with small businesses looking to expand. We will look at a company which does not have significant resources and say "Does it stand a chance of succeeding?" If it does we're willing to gamble. These are normally businesses that could not go to a bank for a loan because they represent too much of a risk. (Newburgh Evening News 8/9/82)

Efforts to get information on the age and size of firms getting RLF funding were unsuccessful. How many of the firms were three years old or younger is unknown, although the director indicated one firm was a true startup. Of the six to ten loans authorized between 1981 and 1982, most went to firms with less than fifty employees. All of the minority loan funds went to one-to-four person businesses in retail and service sectors.

On balance, Orange acted as though it was more interested in assisting and financing businesses for most of the 1975–1980 period. Its IDAs became active earlier and it was the first to have an RLF, albeit rather late in the study period.

Venture Capital. There are no venture capital firms based in either Orange or Dutchess counties. Informants commented that startup capital is hard to find but said that this is true everywhere. In Orange, Louis Heimbach, the county executive, doubted that venture capital was something governments should be involved in since as few as 10 or 20 percent of prospects will succeed. This skepticism about government involvement was reinforced by his belief that the private sector had the most to gain from promoting small, new firms and should take the risks. In Dutchess County venture capital is not seen as an especially critical problem. Venture capital can be brought into the county through ties with New York City banks and their venture capital arms. Even if local developers wanted to get into venture capital, available funding sources are inappropriate to the financing needs of small, new firms (McEnroe interview).

Facilities. Like venture capital, incubator faciities for small firms have not been considered as development tools in these counties. While vacant industrial facilities have been available, they are marketed for reuse in one piece, rather than being divided into industrial condominiums or incubators.

Information

In Orange County, management assistance to small firms consists of periodic small-business startup seminars and Service Corps of Retired Executives (SCORE) programs run by the chambers of commerce. There is no ombudsman per se although the heads of the East Orange (Newburgh) and Orange (Middletown) Chambers of Commerce assist firms with financing and regulatory matters. The director and a staff assistant in the East Orange Chamber spend as much as 50 percent of their time on financial packaging and site selection assistance, mostly for established or proven businesses (Taxter). The director of the East Orange Chamber indicated that most of the firms it worked with had fewer than fifty employees but that most were also older than five years.

Orange County's Director of Planning and Economic Development also troubleshoots problems that firms may have. New firms have access to these services but no special management programs have been created for younger firms. Newburgh provides some management and financial advice, especially for firms using the Minority Venture Capital Loan Fund, but like other development agencies, they do not have the staff to consult with firms on a regular basis.

In Dutchess County, the quasi-public Dutchess County Economic Development Corporation (DCEDC), the lead development agency for the county, periodically sponsors seminars on business operations. A 1981 conference dealt with financing programs available to businesses and a 1982 program with quality circles. DCEDC has occasionally become involved with management consulting, as it relates to financial packaging. An example of this is the effort by the director to guide development of a business plan and financial package to help former employees of Western Publishing Company set up a printing firm after they were put out of work by the closure of the Western operation in Poughkeepsie in 1982.

After this experience with the Western closing, it was suggested that DCEDC assemble a management "SWAT Team" that could assist firms in trouble. Bert Howe, the director of DCEDC, was skeptical of this idea and of the general approach of providing management assistance to any firm that asks for it. His primary criticism was that management problems vary so much by sector and firm that efforts to provide generic management advice would be of little use (Howe interview). Jack McEnroe, president of Dutchess Bank and member of DCEDC's board of directors, stated that the need for management advice occurs so infrequently at the local level that it would not be cost effective to try to maintain the expertise to provide it. When asked whether management advice for young, small firms was justified he argued that in many cases it probably was, citing common management problems his loan officers find. He said such assistance was not now available but maybe it was something DCEDC should consider.

The evidence presented here indicates that technical assistance for small, established firms is more widely available in Orange than in Dutchess, especially on matters of site selection, financial packaging, and troubleshooting regulatory problems. This occurs for two reasons. First, Orange simply has more individuals doing economic development (seven instead of three). Second, Dutchess's developers are more selective in initiating contacts with firms and becoming involved in financing or location decisions. The reason for these differences will be discussed below.

Political Climate

A survey of the Mid-Hudson's economic development potential characterized both Dutchess and Orange as being strongly pro-industry and as actively courting investment. "Either county would welcome any type of industry that did not bring substantial air or water pollution" (Mid-Hudson Patterns for Progress, Inc. 1983). The counties are similar in this general way but they differ in the level of government at which most development efforts occur and in the kind of things they do to create a positive political climate for business.

Orange County

In Orange County two strong chambers of commerce, several townships, and the City of Newburgh carry on most of the development promotion occurring in the county. County government, especially the executive Louis Heimbach, has provided much vocal support for economic development but little financial support. This is partly because the organizations just mentioned have preempted most development tasks and resist the executive's efforts to widen the county's role. Another factor seems to be ideology; government should not take on a task unless absolutely necessary and its effort should nurture desirable activity but not control it. Several examples will be presented to show how these tendencies work together to define development efforts in the county.

In the early 1970s several county leaders wanted to establish an Industrial Development Authority but a debate arose over its powers, management, and its relationship to county government. A Republican state assemblyman from Newburgh held up the county's application for IDA status because he was concerned that cities and towns might lose power compared with the county. His actions reflected the view then apparently held by some in the county that the county was attempting to become a "super-government" by taking on powers best left to municipalities (*Middletown Times Herald Record* 5/30/71, 5/5/72, 11/29/72).

Soon after the IDA was established the question of its physical location came up, and directors of the Orange County (Middletown) Chamber of Commerce offered space and a telephone in its building. Chamber leaders argued that the IDA's financing tools would support and be supported by the chamber's active advertising, site information, and business development efforts. The IDA Board decided against the offer in part because it would associate the IDA (a county agency) too closely with one part of the county. Another consideration was that the IDA's job was not "attracting industry" but providing financial aid. It was the responsibility of the chambers to recruit firms (*Record* 1/24/73). The board reaffirmed this partitioned approach to development later when it used the same reasoning in turning down the director of the county's airport who asked the IDA to help him attract corporate clients to use the airport facilities (*Record* 5/14/73). According to the county's director of planning, the IDA continues to "stick to its knitting" (i.e., approving industrial revenue bonds) (DeTurk interview). The IDA generally waits for prospects to come to it rather than trying to generate business for itself, and it still lacks a full-time staff to work with business prospects.

The IDA is a public authority but the county itself has also been restrained in what it has tried to do to promote development. The county's efforts can be described as trying to limit the growth in tax rates, being sensitive to business's views, and maintaining public support for development and its benefits. The county has not spent large amounts of money for projects benefiting the business community or provided services (e.g., management advice or equity financing) to assist businesses. In short, the county has taken a supportive rather than interventionist approach to promoting development.

In 1981 several county legislators proposed that the county build an industrial park, combining some of its own money with a public works grant from the Economic Development Administration. By 1983 the park still had not been built, in part because of concerns that the county should not compete with private firms by operating such a facility. Some legislators expressed the view that county government would enjoy an unfair advantage in operating such an industrial park (*Record* 2/17/81). Since it is widely acknowledged that the county is handicapped in attracting firms because it lacks a full-service industrial park (Arthur D. Little 1981) this decision shows the depth of the county's commitment to limited government.

County government's economic development policies have been largely defined by Louis Heimbach, the county executive since 1979. In his first campaign he made an issue of increasing economic growth, and he has spent a good deal of time keeping the development issue before the voters and the legislature. In his view Orange County requires no large infusion of public sector resources to improve economic growth or even new development initiatives of any sort. Orange County has a number of advantages in access to markets, transportation links, quality of life, and moderate land, labor, and energy costs. What was needed, he believed, was simply to get the word out to individuals making corporate location decisions about the good things Orange had to offer. His initiatives were in line with his view that the needs are moderate and that government intervention should be limited.[10]

One of his first efforts was to establish a local tax abatement program that would be available to businesses expanding employment. Firms would be eligible for the abatement for three years beyond the ten years of tax forgiveness already available through New York State's 485 and 485b tax abatement programs. He acknowledges that tax abatement creates little new investment but he wanted a low-cost way to convey to the business community that Orange County wanted new business. A second purpose was to use the debate stirred up by the proposal to educate Orange County residents about the benefits of development and to change policies on zoning and tax assessment that he thought were needed and that also inhibited new investment.

For several years the executive has also tried to get business support for creating a county-wide economic development corporation, such as Oneida

County's OCIDC. The purpose of the corporation would be to support an individual who would serve as a "super salesman" (his word) to market Orange County to corporate decision makers outside the county. Other business recruitment and marketing efforts have come out of the Orange County Economic Development Committee, an advisory body maintained with Heimbach's encouragement and leadership. The committee's major activities since 1979 have been: a $25,000 study contracted out to A. D. Little Co. to identify industries that might be interested in expanding in Orange, a $75,000 program of advertising and mailings to contact firms identified by the A. D. Little effort, a slide show to advertise the county's advantages at trade shows and to prosepctive firms, a tour around the county for real estate brokers from New York city who might be in a position to steer firms toward Orange County, and regular breakfasts bringing together government officials and businessmen to discuss mutual concerns (DeTurk interview).[11]

Orange County has been very active on economic development but its efforts provide no direct assistance to a business's operations. County actions are largely informational, in contrast to direct efforts that would make financial and managerial assistance readily available to business. To the extent the latter types of assistance are available in the county, they come from Newburgh and the chambers of commerce, not county government.

Dutchess County. Before the mid–1970s Dutchess County was more concerned with controlling the effects of growth than with promoting it. Development policy had long been shaped by fears that the county would be overtaken by New York City sprawl, such as Westchester experienced. Dutchess County government developed strong land use planning regulations and a highly professional staff to control the growth that did occur. Many communities also zoned large parcels of land as industrial to keep residential development under control. A 1973 editorial in the Poughkeepsie Journal expressed the view that the main concern in development was land use. Planners believed that growth would overwhelm the county and decisions had to be made about the way to channel and control it. Trying to zone it out would not work. (*Poughkeepsie Journal* 8/20/73). At a 1978 conference on economic growth in Dutchess this view still prevailed. Jack McEnroe, president of Dutchess Bank, said "I've never felt so strongly about the fact that Dutchess county is about to 'pop' economically. We're going to get action whether we want it or not, and we'd better be prepared for it" (*Journal* 11/19/78).

Dutchess County did grow but economic conditions in New York were already deteriorating. By 1976 business interests began work to establish an organization to promote economic development in the county, an effort that was strongly supported by both business and public leaders. The Dutchess County Economic Development Corporation (DCEDC) was formally established in 1978 with a $50,000 budget of which the county furnished

$35,000. By 1983 the corporation's budget had grown to $150,000 and the county's share was up to $75,000. Behind the creation of DCEDC lay two concerns. The county could not always rely on IBM to guarantee a healthy economy and Dutchess was losing its manufacturing base outside electronics (textiles, machine tools) (Howe interview). Also, there was interest in trying to plan ahead, to begin recruiting new firms before a crisis developed that forced action. "The idea was to set this up without a crisis and be somewhat selective in the kind of industries that we encourage" (McEnroe interview). Among the targets were industries that fit "the kind of environmental quality that we like to see here" and those that would help alleviate the pockets of unemployment among low-skilled workers in the cities of Poughkeepsie and Beacon (McEnroe interview).

This directive resulted in DCEDC being concerned primarily with helping existing local firms expand and with recruiting new firms into the community. In implementing these objectives, Bert Howe, director of DCEDC, prefers that the corporation keep a low profile enabling it to move on development opportunities that he and his staff identify. DCEDC is not trying to be a business development service for every firm in the county but seeks to use staff expertise and public development incentives selectively where they can make a difference in a business's operations or in a location decision.

The county executive, Lucille Pattison, elected in 1979, has been extremely supportive of the corporation's activities. The county contributes up to half the corporation's budget and Pattison has worked with Howe on the effort to save Western Publishing. The county executive also supported economic development by creating a "one-stop" permit office in 1981 and by pushing for a hotel room tax. The tax, ultimately passed in 1983, was to be used for tourist promotion, and the program would be managed by the Development Corporation.

Aside from DCEDC, which is the lead development body in the county, only Poughkeepsie carries on any development promotion activities. Poughkeepsie was very active in urban redevelopment in the 1960's, succeeding in getting Urban Renewal grants to clear large tracts of land. Much land was cleared, but few takers were found. With the advent of the Community Development Block Grant and Urban Development Action Grants the city increased its efforts to redevelop the downtown into a shopping and office location. Approximately $3.5 million was spent turning a downtown street into an open shopping plaza and another $2 million to build a large public parking garage adjacent to it. In 1981 a $1.5 million UDAG was won for an office building in this same downtown mall area. The mayor was instrumental in convincing IBM to locate some of its employees in the building; previously the company had no operations within the city at all. Repayments on the UDAG would be used for further economic development activity, perhaps a revolving loan fund (Bersak interview). The city also made numerous efforts in the latter of 1970s to win another UDAG to help construct a hotel along the Hudson near the other downtown developments. This effort has been unsuccessful. Nevertheless, the director of planning for the city emphasized in citing such activities that, "the city is *not* indifferent" to the business community and economic development concerns. Unlike Newburgh, however, Poughkeepsie does not provide economic development or business assistance services within the structure of the city government. On a question about working with business, the director of planning for the city replied that contacting firms is the function of the chambers of commerce and DCEDC, not the City of Poughkeepsie.

Economic development efforts have been relatively unaffected by disputes between elected officials or between elected officials and developers. Disagreements did occur between the city and town of Poughkeepsie when the former refused to supply water to the faster-growing town, but generally the county seems to have amicable relations among its jurisdictions. Similarly, relations between DCEDC and the Chambers of Commerce of Poughkeepsie and Beacon are also peaceable, if not especially close. DCEDC has worked with the chambers of commerce when JDA financing is brought into a financial package since the chambers are authorized to approve JDA loans while the development corporation is not. DCEDC and the chambers also worked together to try and keep Western Publishing open. The chambers are not as active in recruiting new firms or helping local firms to expand as are the two chambers in Orange.

Economic development seems to be more tightly run than in Orange County but this is primarily the effect of the smaller number of actors involved and the agreement that participants share about the purposes of economic development in the county. The county should seek out development that will maintain the healthy local economy while being careful not to damage the environmental and cultural qualities of life that make Dutchess attractive. The county is most certainly not distressed, despite losing some old-line firms, and has chosen to take a more relaxed and selective approach to development.

IMPLICATIONS FOR BUSINESS STARTS

Oneida and Niagara offer a good test of the entrepreneurial model. Oneida has been energetic, fairly innovative, and risk-oriented in its development promotion efforts. Niagara, in contrast, has established the groundwork for small business promotion but in the 1975–1982 period had little to offer small, new firms. If resources and political climate do influence business startup decisions we should see an increase in the rate of startups in Oneida after 1978 while little change occurs in Niagara.

Dutchess and Orange are not as neat opposites of each other. Orange has more organizations and individuals promoting development than Dutchess, financial packaging and location assistance seem more widely available, and Newburgh did initiate an innovative development effort incorporating some of the ideas discussed in earlier chapters. Activity on the municipal level is balanced by a reticence on the part of the county government to become deeply involved in providing development services to businesses. To say the county is inactive or uninterested in development is wrong, but its chosen methods cannot be called innovative using the definitions presented earlier. The interesting empirical question is whether making development a visible issue and showing appreciation for business's views in the absence of substantive actions to assist business operations leads entrepreneurs to start up more firms. The argument presented earlier would suggest the answer is no.

The level of development promotion in Dutchess clearly increased in the later 1970s. Its methods, however, are not innovative by the definition being used here. Moreover, while the county has supported DCEDC financially and on particular projects, the overall level of activity was more subdued and selective in its targets than in Orange. DCEDC and the city of Poughkeepsie simply did not have the staff to carry on wide-ranging development efforts. Finally, the policy of DCEDC and officials involved in development is that development efforts should be selective. As a result, information about financing and managerial advice are probably less widely available than in Orange. Based on the level of policy effort alone, we would expect little change in the rate of business startups in the county in the later 1970s.

NOTES

1. A figure of 1.1 indicates that employment is 10 percent higher than in 1970; one of 0.9 indicates that employment is 10 percent lower.

2. Between 1977 and 1982 the civilian labor force in Niagara grew 2.5 percent while employment declined 3.6 percent. Oneida's employment also fell (0.1 percent) but its labor force fell more (0.6 percent) which lowered its unemployment rate. Dutchess and Orange created new jobs at much faster rates, 17.7 percent and 7.6 percent respectively. Both were able to lower their unemployment rates because the civilian labor force was not growing as rapidly, 17.7 percent in Dutchess and 6.1 percent in Orange (New York State SUNY Albany 1983).

3. Outside manufacturing, smaller percentages of loans go to very young firms. While 58 percent of the nineteen manufacturing loans went to firms three years old or younger, only thirty-two percent of the thirty-three retail loans went to firms of that age. A possible explanation is that RLF monies originate in HUD's community development funds, a major purpose of which is to improve downtowns and established retail strips. When used in this setting, established firms are the major beneficiaries.

4. The creation of these RLFs reflected a widespread awareness among business people and government officials that Oneida County badly needed risk-oriented venture capital. As early as 1973 members of OCIDC's board discussed the idea of setting up a $250,000 venture capital fund. Utica board members who raised the

issue "felt that there is a dire need for this kind of front money to start incubator firms up in our area" (OCIDC Minutes 3/26/73).

5. Part of the explanation for these differences is that the average size of firms in Niagara is larger than it is in Oneida. Niagara manufacturing firms have an average of 103 employees compared with Oneida's sixty-nine. The number of firms with fewer than twenty employees is about the same, however: 128 in Niagara to 108 in Oneida (*County Business Patterns* 1981). Without a conscious effort to solicit interest from smaller firms, NCIDA is likely to get larger firms than would approach OCIDC in Oneida. The other reason, of course, is that small firms simply cannot make use of IRBs to any great extent.

6. This program has been specifically cited by HUD as not conforming to national CDBG guidelines for 51 percent of the benefit going to low-and moderate-income individuals. Rome calculated the benefit by averaging across all projects while HUD requires the benefit to be calculated separately for each project. HUD's interpretation greatly limits the discretion of communities in determining the kind and timing of investments they make.

7. The county had received state funding to set up a small-business assistance center (modeled on those funded by the SBA at universities around the country). Several sources in the county mentioned the center as the primary source for management advice in the county when it became operational in late 1983.

8. On Orange, for example, see "The Wooing of Wakefern," *Middletown Times Herald Record* 8/19/79); and "Orange County is Shopping for Business" (*Record* 9/15/80).

9. As of mid–1984 the city had not decided whether these loans would be repaid and turned into a revolving loan fund.

10. This view is disputed by informants in the Newburgh area who feel that county government should be doing more to develop their depressed area. The county was criticized for using Newburgh as a "dumping ground for welfare clients" and for not doing more to transform Stewart Airport (a former air force base) into a transportation hub. The executive commented that it is not right for the county to favor one part of the county more than others.

11. The funding for these activities came from the Industrial Development Authority and the Private Industry Council, the successor to Comprehensive Employment and Training Act (CETA). No money came from the county.

Chapter 6

The Performance of Entrepreneurial Promotion Policies

This chapter presents evidence on how government policy affects small business birthrates. Measurement of business birthrate is discussed along with an evaluation of the quality of the data used to measure births. The results of this study in the New York case study counties will then be presented. Attention is focused on the years 1980 and 1982, when the policies installed in Oneida and Orange are expected to show their effects.[1]

MEASURING BUSINESS STARTUPS

Data was collected on business births in selected manufacturing and service industries. Twenty-four manufacturing SICs (Standard Industrial Classification) were subdivided into the following categories: high technology, small business dominated, and mature manufacturing. Twenty-seven service industry SICs were grouped into: personal services, wholesaling, and business services. Between seven and fourteen three-digit SICs were contained in each industry grouping. The individual SIC titles making up these groupings and the sources for identifying them are described in Appendix E.

Industries are grouped this way to see whether there are differences in the way entrepreneurs respond by industry. High technology industries and wholesaling have high startup rates, and new firms may emerge quite rapidly in these industries in response to policy changes. Mature manufacturing industries may be slower to respond to policy change, or may not respond at all, since they generally exhibit lower birthrates. Personal services may not respond very quickly since they depend more on the health and wealth of the immediate trading area, which are both difficult to affect by local policy initiatives alone.

The dependent variable collected for these industries was the business birthrate. It was calculated with the following formula:

$$\text{Birthrate} = \frac{\text{Firms 0 or 1 years old in SIC} \times 1{,}000}{\text{Employees in SIC}}$$

Dun and Bradstreet Corporation (D & B) records for selected three-digit SICs in the years 1976, 1978, 1980, and 1982 were scanned to identify the number of firms whose business age was 0 or 1 years.[2] This number (measured births) was divided by the number of employees in that three-digit SIC in 1975 (for 1976 and 1978 birth years) and in 1979 (for 1980 and 1982 birth years).[3] The result was then multiplied by 1,000, giving the number of firms created per 1,000 employees.

This approach to measuring entrepreneurial behavior was used because the number of businesses started in an industry is strongly related to the amount of activity already taking place in that industry in the area. To fairly compare births in different locations it was important to control for the size of the industry already there. Employment was used as the base because it most accurately represents the source of spinoffs: individuals already employed in the industry and living in the region.[4] Other methods of measuring births have been used (Birley 1984) but this is the most theoretically sound approach (Cross 1981; Gudgin 1978).

DATA ON BUSINESS STARTS: A QUALITY CHECK

Several data bases contain information useful for studying new firms. (For a detailed comparison of the ones to be mentioned see Harris 1981; SBA 1982; SBA 1983.) *County Business Patterns* (CBP) records contain some of the needed data. CBP data come from a sample of firms by geographical area and are very accurate. Government secrecy regulations prevent data on individual firms from being published, however. Publicly available data only provides information on aggregate numbers of firms by industry. It is impossible to tell, by looking at year-to-year changes in the number of firms, how many firms were created or died.

Internal Revenue Service tax records are available for self-employed individuals, proprietorships, partnerships, and corporations and contain information on a firm's date of incorporation, income, and profit and loss. If IRS records were matched with information maintained by the Social Security Administration, we would have information about a firm's size, its employment growth history, and the racial and sexual makeup of its work force. The raw data in these files are kept strictly confidential, however. Even the Small Business Administration (SBA) has been unable to find an acceptable way to access these records.

Unemployment Insurance (UI) data on firms are generated as part of the administration of the state unemployment insurance system. UI records cover 98 percent of the wage and salary labor force. The reliability of the data is recognized to be very high and has improved in recent years as states have moved to standardize reporting procedures and methods of classifying firms by industry (SBA 1983). Information on individual firms is available to states for purposes of tracking firms. Using these data to study business activity is hampered by the fact that the data are maintained by fifty different states.

In an effort to develop a workable data base on small business, the SBA has purchased files from the Dun and Bradstreet Corporation maintained as an adjunct to its credit reporting services. Reasonably complete records are available starting in 1969. The SBA has put together several types of files from this data base, one of which, the U.S. Enterprise and Establishment Microdata File (USEEM), is used in this study.

The USEEM is developed from Dun's Market Identifier (DMI) files and includes a variety of data for each firm (SBA 1984, 413).

1. Business name and street address
2. Geographic location—city, county, SMSA, state
3. Year in which business started and hence the age of the business to date
4. Annual sales volume (gross sales)
5. Standard Industrial Classification (SIC) code—primary and up to five additional SIC codes
6. Parent firm of establishment and city and state of headquarters
7. Status indicator to denote if establishment is a (1) headquarters, (2) subsidiary, (3) branch, or (4) a single establishment or independent business
8. Indication if manufacturing takes place at this location

USEEM contains records for the years 1976, 1978, 1980, and 1982 that can be accessed for any level of geographic aggregation. Included are approximately 20 million individual records. Altogether, the USEEM offers a detailed profile of the business population. USEEM is useful for this study because it provides information on firm age, which allows birthrates for individual jurisdictions to be calculated.

The DMI and the USEEM derived from it are not without problems. The file is neither a census of all firms nor a sample. Firms enter Dun's files when they engage in financial transactions, e.g., seeking loans or insurance. The SBA observes that " . . . in today's economy, this encompasses most firms involved in full-time business venture," yet USEEM is still a biased representation of the population of U.S. businesses. Firms without employees are not covered, for example (SBA 1984, 412). Compared to Unemployment Insurance records and *County Business Patterns* the USEEM overstates the number of employees in Mining, Finance and Real Estate, and Services by as much as 50 percent. Meanwhile, the average difference between CBP and UI employment counts was less than 3 percent. Reasons

Table 6.1
Alternative Estimates of Business Starts in the United States (1980)

Source	Estimated Annual Starts
Conventional Wisdom	400,000
D & B Business Starts*	390,000
D & B New Incorporations*	3,400,000
Illinois ROT Data I*	1,810,000
Illinois ROT Data II*	2,620,000

Source: Star and Narayana 1983: 48

*Projected to U.S. from Illinois data

for the larger differences between USEEM and the other data series include broader coverage by USEEM, specific reporting practices or options of *County Business Patterns* and UI, or industrial classification patterns, especially those applied to imputed branches by USEEM (Harris 1981, 23).

USEEM's estimate of the number of business startups also differs from estimates based on other data sources. Alvin D. Star and Chem L. Narayana compared D & B's business starts estimate to those derived from four other sources: (1) Conventional Wisdom, (2) Dun & Bradstreet new incorporation data, (3) Illinois Retailers' occupational tax data adjusted with census data, and (4) Illinois retailers' occupational tax data adjusted with Department of Commerce and Internal Revenue Service data (1983, 45). Table 6.1 indicates that Dun and Bradstreet's data may understate the true number of starts by up to seven times. Star and Narayana conclude that policy makers may be misled about the amount of turnover in the business population if they rely on D & B data. They are concerned that the "use of the Dun & Bradstreet file data base might incorrectly signal less need for startups assistance or pretermination support when, in fact, more assistance was required " (1983, 48).

One further point should be noted about the extract from USEEM used in this study. On the advice of SBA officials it omits firms with imputed data in their records. That is, firms which exist and were detected by D & B are left out if they had incorrect or missing data that were estimated or corrected by the Brookings Institution in preparing the raw data for the SBA (Harris 1981, 1982). The effect of this is that the count of new firms derived from this study probably understates the number of new firms detected by D & B which in turn certainly understates the number of firms actually started.

D & B's coverage is very good in some sectors (e.g., manufacturing) and very poor in others (e.g., wholesaling and services). Fortunately, of the six industry groupings used in the analyses below, only one, personal services,

Table 6.2
Correlation of D & B and UI Count of Firms in New York Counties: Age 0

	Correlation (R)			
	1976	1978	1980	1982
Dutchess	.75	.21	.18	.22
Niagara	.85	.47	.50	.70
Oneida	.67	.00*	.61	.09
Orange	.47	.32	.21	.35

* D & B recorded no firms Age 0
  in Oneida for 1978

is seriously affected by D & B undercounting. The others, high technology, small firm dominated industries, mature manufacturing, business services, and wholesaling, utilize SIC groupings where D & B coverage is strongest. Appendix E describes the SIC groupings used.

Understatement alone is not too serious if it exists to the same degree over time and from one location to another. Unfortunately this may not be the case. D & B's coverage of business activity has improved in recent years (SBA 1984), which could create the impression that births increased when all that happened is that the coverage improved. This possibility was investigated by comparing D & B's count of firms age 0 years in 1976 through 1982 to birth counts obtained from unemployment insurance records. When available, unemployment insurance records offer a very complete record of business operations, including startups. Since 1976 New York State has used its UI data to track changes in the state's business population at the individual firm level. Data was available at the two-digit SIC level on business startups for selected New York counties.[5]

Table 6.2 displays the results of correlating D & B and UI counts of firms aged 0. Except for Niagara, D & B's ability to detect startups in the year they occurred actually declined after 1976 as indicated by the weaker correlation coefficients in more recent years. Inter-year correlations of starts reported by UI in these counties are in the .8 to .9 range, indicating that UI detected similar numbers of starts during these years. Inter-year correlations using D & B data, on the other hand, vary from .15 to .85 (figures not shown). This indicates that the number of births detected by D & B varies much more from year to year than the number detected by the presumably more reliable UI system.

In an attempt to make the D & B data usable, firms 0 or 1 years old in a year were counted as starts for that year. That is, a firm born in 1975 or 1976 was considered a 1976 start. The justification is that businessmen's perception of the local policy climate would not change much between

Table 6.3
Correlation of D & B and UI Count of Firms in New York Counties: Age 0
or 1

	Correlation (R)			
	1976	1978	1980	1982
Dutchess	.75	.51	.43	.39
Niagara	.91	.75	.57	.67
Oneida	.75	.48	.62	.41
Orange	.53	.61	.34	.46

adjoining years and, therefore, starts in either year can be considered equiv-
alent for purposes of testing policy impacts.

How does this measure of starts compare with the one derived from UI
data? Table 6.3 displays correlations between D & B's count for firms 0 or
1 years old and UI's record of new firms born in a year. Adding firms a
year old to D & B's counts brings the total closer to UI's but there are still
differences in the number of young firms detected.

Another way to compare these data sets is to see whether D & B con-
sistently understates or overstates births in different SICs and how this
changed between 1976 and 1982. These time points, being six years apart,
should reveal changes in coverage if it occurs. Figures 6.1 through 6.4 chart
the difference between the number of births recorded by D & B and UI in
four New York study counties.[6] The higher the peak, the more D & B
understates UI's count of firms. Negative values indicate that D & B recorded
more firms for an SIC than UI. Values clustered around 0 indicate that the
two data sets contain similar numbers of firms in an SIC.

The difference plots for the two years track each other rather closely,
indicating that D & B's coverage did not change greatly in this six-year
period. This is important because it means that changes in birthrates cannot
be explained away by changes in D & B's coverage. Exceptions occur in
Dutchess and Niagara where several manufacturing, transportation, and
wholesaling SICs saw undercounting by D & B in 1976 turn into over-
counting by 1982. This would make it seem as though more growth had
occurred in these sectors than is warranted based on the data from UI
records.

These differences between UI and D & B data series do not occur because
the data sets systematically exclude different kinds of firms in the sectors
examined here. UI excludes firms that are irrelevant in this research: rail
transportation, non-profit organizations with fewer than four employees,
private household workers, proprietors, self-employed and unpaid family
workers. D & B does not systematically exclude any workers or firms but
most sole-proprietors and partnerships without paid employees are omitted

Figure 6.1
Dutchess: Difference between UI and D & B Counts of New Firms

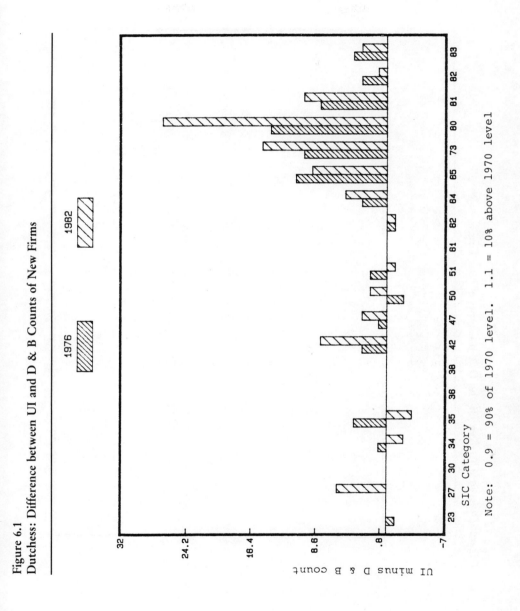

Note: 0.9 = 90% of 1970 level. 1.1 = 10% above 1970 level

Figure 6.2
Niagara: Difference between UI and D & B Counts of New Firms

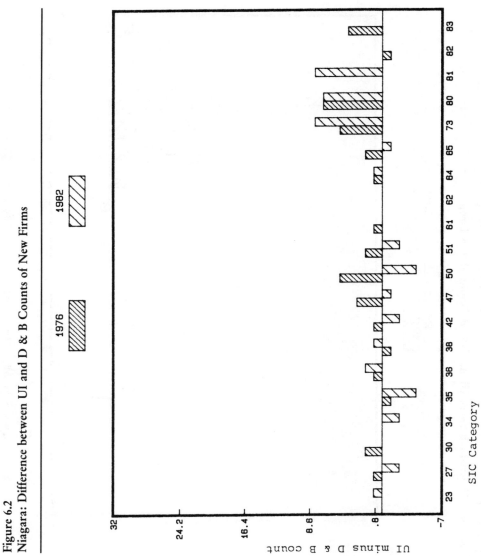

Figure 6.3
Oneida: Difference between UI and D & B Counts of New Firms

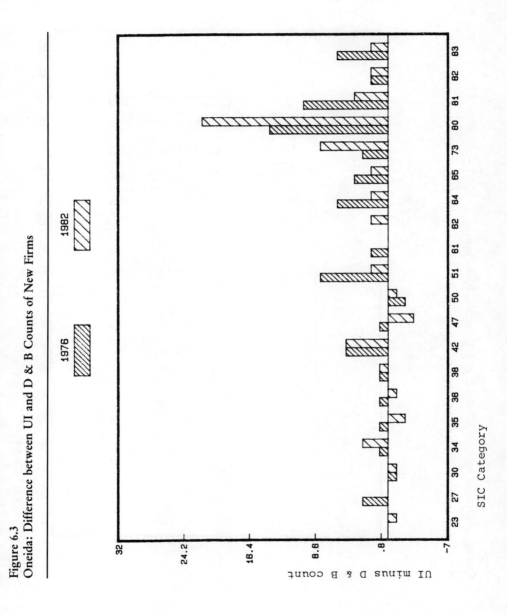

Figure 6.4
Orange: Difference between UI and D & B Counts of New Firms

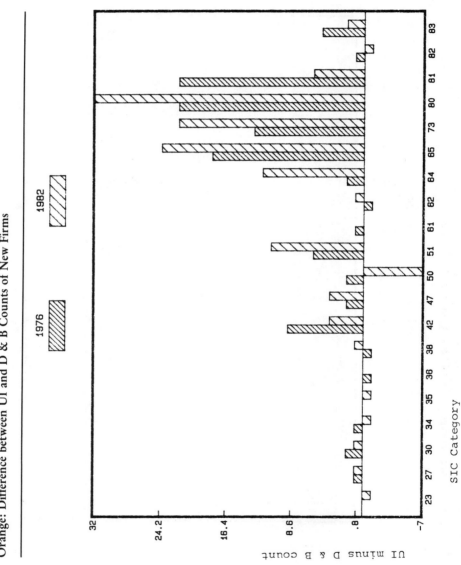

(Harris 1982, 4). D & B's exclusion of some firms without paid employees should not be a factor in coverage because these firms would not enter the Unemployment Insurance data base either.

The most plausible explanation for the differences in coverage is that the demand for credit ratings among very young firms varies a great deal from year to year. If firms do not engage in financial transactions requiring commercial credit ratings then D & B would not detect them. Since firms in service sectors require less startup capital than manufacturing firms, fewer would need a formal credit rating.

Whatever the reasons for the differences, they have serious implications for the analysis of business births. Ideally, D & B data would be able to record a good proportion of births in the year they occur. This does not happen and the solution developed here of counting ages 0 or 1 as births is not really satisfactory. While it does produce higher and less variable correlations with births recorded by UI, it injects measurement error into the data. The startup decision of a 1979 birth, for example, may have begun in 1978, while the entrepreneur behind a 1980 startup may have only looked at the local policy climate in the latter part of 1980. So much time between decision points makes it harder to say they are responding to the same political climates.

EVIDENCE ON BIRTHRATES

Two measures of business activity were examined: (1) mean birthrates in 1980 and 1982 in the six industry groupings; and (2) change scores calculated by subtracting mean 1978 and 1980 birthrates from mean 1980 and 1982 birthrates, respectively. The key independent variable is the county where a particular SIC birthrate was recorded, whether a high or low policy effort site or a baseline county. The findings for the distressed counties (Oneida and Niagara) will be discussed first and then those for the growing counties (Dutchess and Orange).

Distressed and growing counties were analyzed separately because it was expected that underlying rates of birth would be higher in growing counties than in distressed counties. The only fair test of the entrepreneurial model would be to compare counties with similar levels of economic health. In addition, the two high policy effort sites (Oneida and Orange) had not promoted small business with the same intensity. Since Oneida's effort was clearly the most innovative of the four counties it was analyzed separately in order not to dilute the possible impact of its policies by averaging its observed birthrates with those in Orange.

Note that the unit of analysis is the SIC, not the county. Entrepreneurs who began firms in an SIC were considered to have been exposed to different policy treatments in the high, low, and baseline policy effort counties. One reason for using the SIC rather than the county as the unit of analysis was to increase the degrees of freedom for the statistical analyses. In addition, this approach more accurately reflects the industry as a population of firms responding to environmental change. It is possible that different industry populations could react differently to the same policy change.

Initial analysis of birth levels was done with the general linear model using the specification:

$$B(t) = L + B(t-2) + L \times B(t-2)$$

Where:

$B(t)$ = Mean birthrates in 1980 or 1982
L = Location (Categorical variable identifying a birthrate score as coming from a high or low policy effort county, or a baseline county)
$B(t-2)$ = Mean birthrate in 1978 or 1980
$L \times B(t-2)$ = Interaction of birthrate and location

This equation tests the hypothesis that county location (policy effort) explains birthrates after controlling for previous birth levels. The interaction term, $L \times B(t-2)$, tests for parallel regression slopes. If this coefficient is significant it means that birthrates do not respond in the same way in different counties. Births at $t-2$ were used in the model to control for a possible relationship between birthrates and unmeasured local factors.[7] Change scores were analyzed using only location, since birthrate at $t-2$ was used to calculate the change score and could not be used as a separate independent variable.

Distressed Counties: Birth Levels

The analysis of distressed counties included the following counties: High Policy Effort (Oneida, N.Y.), Low Policy Effort (Niagara, N.Y.), Baseline Counties (Kalamazoo and Saginaw, Mich.; Lackawanna and Northampton, Pa.; and Broome, N.Y.). Table 6.4 presents partial F scores ($p = .10$) for the analysis of 1980 and 1982 birthrates for distressed counties using the full model. A partial F gives the significance of a particular variable in explaining the dependent variable while controlling for the other variables in the equation.

The location variable (L) summarizes the overall effect of location (county) on birthrates.[8] Whether we can say that policy effort caused the pattern of the F scores in the "L" column depends on the specific pattern of birthrates in the three types of counties.

One important thing to note in Table 6.4 is that location accounts for significant amounts of variance in high technology, mature manufacturing, small business, and wholesaling sectors in 1980. Location fails to make an independent contribution to births in any sector in 1982.

Note, too, that the conditions apparently changed between 1978 and 1980–

Table 6.4
Effect of Location and Prior Birth Levels on Birthrates: Niagara and Oneida Counties

	Partial F (p <=.10)			
Births (1980) =	L	B(1978) +	L*B(1978)	R^2
Business Svcs.				
High Tech. Manuf.	2.79 (.07)			.07
Mature Manuf.	4.9 (.01)	14.5 (.0003)	9.54 (.003)	.36
Personal Svcs.				
Small Firm Manuf.	3.3 (.04)			.09
Wholes.	3.6 (.04)			.22
Births (1982) =	L	B(1980) +	L*B(1980)	R^2
Business Svcs.		7.39 (.01)	2.45 (.10)	.89
High Tech. Manuf.			168.9 (.0001)	.94
Mature Manuf.		88.8 (.0001)	38.6 (.0001)	.64
Personal Svcs.		3.3 (.08)	17.3 (.0001)	.64
Small Firm Manuf.		97.0 (.0001)	28.3 (.0001)	.60
Wholes.				

B   = Birthrate
L   = Location (case study or baseline county)
L*B = Interaction Term

1982. In 1980 location is important in explaining births in four industry groupings while 1978 births or the interaction term are significant in only one grouping. By 1982, birthrates or birthrates interacting with location were significant in five of the six industry groupings while location alone was not significant in any. This indicates that level of birth activity changed in some of the counties between 1978 and 1980 and leveled off from then until 1982. Birthrates in 1980 helped explain 1982 births, indicating that birth activity did not change much between these years. Birthrates in 1978, on the other hand, were not useful in explaining 1980 births while location was, indicating that something unique occurred in one or more of the counties between 1978 and 1980 to significantly change the level of birth activity. Since location stands for policy differences, this may mean that policy is having an impact on entrepreneurs' startup decisions between 1978 and 1980.

To determine whether policy effort helps explain these findings, the variance explained by location was partitioned into components associated with specific contrasts: Oneida-vs-Niagara, Oneida-vs-Baseline, and Niagara-vs-Baseline. Partitioning variance into components helps to determine which pair of locations had significantly different mean birthrates. The entrepreneurial model would suggest that Oneida should experience significantly higher mean birthrates than either Niagara or the baseline counties in 1980 and 1982. The larger the difference between two sites, the more that pair would contribute to explaining the variance of the birthrate variable. If Oneida's birthrate was higher and significantly different from the one in Niagara and the Baseline Counties, we could have more confidence that policy effort was in fact affecting entrepreneurial behavior in these counties. (For a discussion of the partitioning procedure, see Kleinbaum and Kupper 1978, 277–83; and SAS 1982, 146–47.)

Table 6.5 presents F values ($p = .10$) for contrasts between the two case study counties and the baseline average. A significant F value indicates that mean birthrate in one type of county was significantly different from the mean birthrate in the contrasted county. Significant differences between Oneida and Niagara occur in mature manufacturing and wholesaling in 1980. However, it was not Oneida's birthrate that was higher, but Niagara's (see Figures 6.5 and 6.6).

Niagara's good performance in wholesaling should be discounted since part of its increase is the result of measurement error discussed earlier. The method of counting births produced higher counts for Niagara than probably occurred, judging by UI records.

Table 6.5 also shows that the contrast between Oneida and the baseline was significant for high technology manufacturing and small firms industries in 1980 and for high technology manufacturing in 1982. Oneida's most consistent improvement occurred in high technology. As can be seen in Figure 6.7, Oneida improved its birthrates over both Niagara and the baseline average, but its performance did not improve enough to make it sig-

Table 6.5
Effect of Location on Mean Birthrates: Oneida and Niagara Counties

| | F Value (p <=.10) | | | | | |
| | Oneida-Niagara | | Oneida-Baseline | | Niagara-Baseline | |
	1980	1982	1980	1982	1980	1982
Business Services						
High Tech. Manuf.			3.2** (.08)	4.6** (.04)		
Mature Manuf.	4.7* (.03)			12.2* (.001)		
Personal Services						
Small Firm Manuf.			6.95** (.01)			
Wholes.	9.7* (.003)				17.0* (.0001)	6.3* (.02)

* Niagara's birthrate was higher
** Oneida's birthrate was higher

nificantly different from Niagara at the .10 level. (The F score for the contrast between them in 1980 was 2.7, p = .11 and in 1982 2.2, p = .13.) Oneida's performance in small firm manufacturing was very good in 1980, but it fell back just as dramatically in 1982 (see Figure 6.8). In 1982 Niagara's birthrate in wholesaling was significantly different from the baseline but not from Oneida's.

Summarizing the results, Oneida's mean level of births was not significantly higher than Niagara's in any industry or year, although it was higher than the baseline average in two industries in 1980 and one in 1982. The expectation that entrepreneurs in high birthrate industries (high technology and wholesaling) would respond quickly to policy change and begin new firms is not confirmed by these data. These findings also fail to support the expectations of the entrepreneurial model. Oneida's more innovative efforts failed to produce significantly higher birthrates than Niagara in any industry. The fact that Oneida's birthrate was higher than the baseline average in two industries without also being higher than Niagara's probably indicates that

Figure 6.5
Mature Manufacturing Startups: Distressed Counties

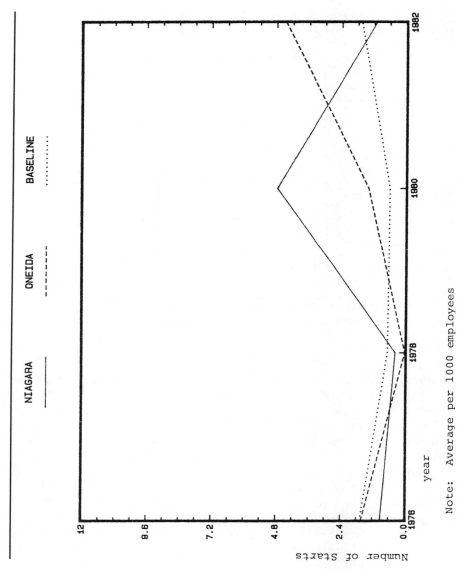

Note: Average per 1000 employees

Figure 6.6
Wholesaling Startups: Distressed Counties

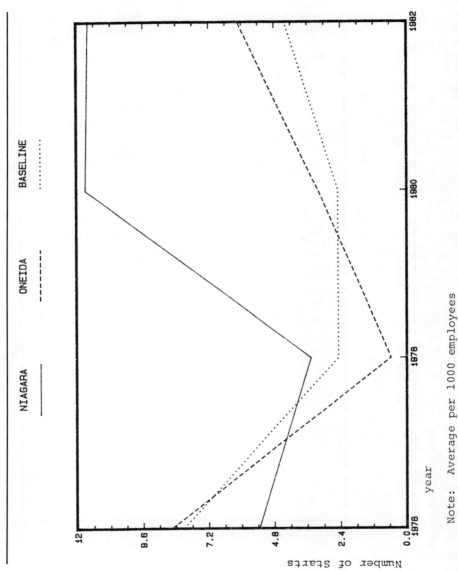

NIAGARA ────────   ONEIDA ─ ─ ─ ─   BASELINE ·········

Note: Average per 1000 employees

Figure 6.7
High Technology Startups: Distressed Counties

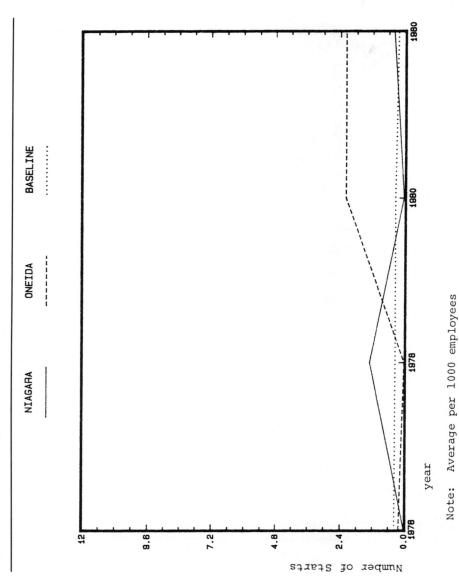

Note: Average per 1000 employees

Figure 6.8
Small Firm Manufacturing Startups: Distressed Counties

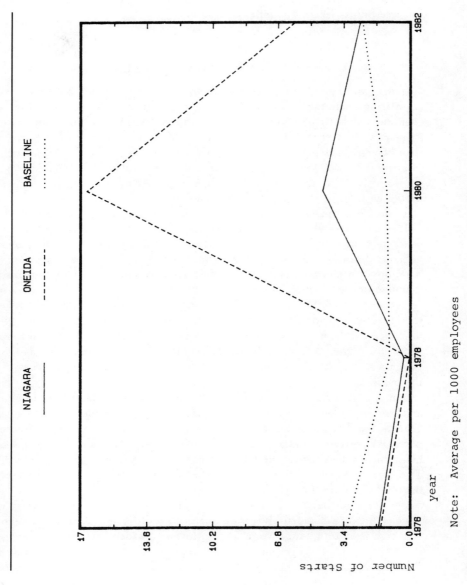

Note: Average per 1000 employees

New York State's economic climate was better than that in other Northern states for these industries. Oneida did better than similar counties elsewhere but not so well as to be considered significantly better than Niagara. In short, policy effort does not seem to be having an impact on birth activity in these industries and counties.

Distressed Counties: Birthrate Change Scores

It may be that Oneida's births are naturally lower than Niagara's and comparing their mean levels of births is inappropriate. Another way to examine Oneida's performance is to compare the *increase* in its births to Niagara's. To test the hypothesis that Oneida improved significantly more than Niagara, a change score analysis was employed (Reichardt 1979). Birthrates in 1978 and 1980 were subtracted from the rates for 1980 and 1982, respectively. The differences were then analyzed using the general linear model with location as a single independent variable.

Table 6.6 displays the significant F values for the change score analysis. Values are listed when one location's increase in birthrates was significantly different from another's change in birthrates. Table 6.6 shows that Oneida had significant increases in births compared with both Niagara and the baseline counties only in high technology industries in 1978–1980. In mature manufacturing Oneida had a significant increase in births compared to Niagara in 1980–1982 but its increase was not significantly different from the baseline. Oneida had a significant increase in births compared with the baseline average in small manufacturing in 1978–1980, but it was not significantly higher than Niagara's. One should also note that in 1978–1980 Niagara's rapid growth in mature manufacturing outpaced both Oneida and the baseline.

Summarizing the change score results, of the three cases where Oneida and Niagara experienced significantly different rates of increase in births, Oneida was higher in one and Niagara in two. These results indicate that potential entrepreneurs in the higher effort counties did not respond to favorable policies within the first two years of the programs being in place. The entrepreneurial model suggests that Oneida should have had higher birthrates in more industries than Niagara.

On the other hand, it is interesting to note that the only classification in which Oneida's change in birthrate outpaced both Niagara and the baseline was high technology industries. This industry was identified earlier as being the one most likely to respond quickly to policy changes. This may indicate that Oneida's entrepreneurial efforts were having an impact on decision making in this rapidly changing industry. The time horizon is shorter in this industry and potential entrepreneurs may be quicker to respond to changes in their environment.

Table 6.6
Effect of Location on Change Scores: Oneida and Niagara Counties

| | F Value (p <=.10) | | | | | |
| | Oneida-Niagara | | Oneida-Baseline | | Niagara-Baseline | |
	1978 /80	1980 /82	1978 /80	1980 /82	1978 /80	1980 /82
Business Services		4.1* (.05)				8.5* (.006)
High Tech. Manuf.	6.1** (.02)		5.4** (.02)			
Mature Manuf.	6.8* (.01)	7.8* (.007)			19.3* (.0001)	
Personal Services						
Small Firm Manuf.			7.5** (.008)			
Wholes.				7.8* (.007)		

* Niagara's increase was steeper
** Oneida's increase was steeper

Growing Counties: Birth Levels

The analyses of growing counties included the following counties: High Policy Effort (Orange, N.Y.), Low Policy Effort (Dutchess, N.Y.), Baseline Counties (Washtenaw, Mich.; Beaver, Pa.; and Lorrain, Lake, Butler, and Trumbull, Ohio).

In growing counties policy differences have little impact on the level of births. In an analysis of variance using location, births at $t-2$, and the interaction term, location proved to be significant in only two industries, mature manufacturing and wholesaling in 1980 and wholesaling in 1982 (see Table 6.7, which displays partial F values significant at the .10 level).

Using different specifications of the equation with the general linear model revealed that prior birth levels are even more significant than suggested by the figures in Table 6.7. This is because multicollinearity exists between Births $(t-2)$ and the Location $\times$ Births$(t-2)$ interaction term, which reduces the amount of variance each explains when both are used in the same equa-

Table 6.7
Effect of Location and Prior Birth Levels on Birthrates: Dutchess and Orange Counties

Partial F
(p <= .10)

Births(1980) =	L	+	B(1978)	+	L*B(1978)	R^2
Business Svcs.			14.6 (.0004)			.41
High Tech. Manuf.						
Mature Manuf.	2.78 (.07)		4.9 (.03)			.15
Personal Svcs.			6.8 (.01)			.17
Small Firm Manuf			3.8 (.06)			.12
Wholes.	3.5 (.04)					.19

Births(1982) =	L	+	B(1980)	+	L*B(1980)	R^2
Business Svcs.			12.6 (.001)			.69
High Tech. Manuf.						
Mature Manuf.			33.3 (.001)		6.7 (.002)	.36
Personal Svcs.			27.9 (.0001)		6.7 (.002)	.34
Small Firm Manuf.			7.1 (.009)		2.4 (.10)	.27
Wholes.	2.5 (.09)				6.03 (.004)	.18

B   = Birthrate
L   = Location (case study or baseline county)
L*B = Interaction Term

Table 6.8
Effect of Location and Birthrate Two Years Earlier: Dutchess and Orange Counties

	F Value (p)					
		1980 Births			1982 Births	
	L	B(1978)	R2	L	B(1980)	R2
Bus. Svcs.		30.9 (.0001)	.40		98.2 (.0001)	.62
High Tech. Manuf.			.02		31.8 (.0001)	.26
Mature Manuf.	2.6 (.08)	5.6 (.02)	.14		22.7 (.0001)	.24
Personal Svcs.		9.7 (.003)	.15		13.2 (.0006)	.24
Small Bus. Manuf.		5.4 (.02)	.06		20.9 (.0001)	.23
Wholes.	2.9 (.06)	7.3 (.009)	.16		3.1 (.08)	.04

B = Birthrate
L = Location (case study or baseline county)

tion. This falsely indicates that previous birth levels are insignificant. Dropping the interaction term increased the F value generated by birthrate $(t-2)$ with only a slight loss of overall explanatory power (see Table 6.8). Birthrates at $t-2$ proved to be significant in every industry except high technology in 1980. Policy effort was significant in only two industries in 1980 (mature manufacturing and wholesaling) and significant in none in 1982 (see Table 6.8). What this means is that in most industry groupings there are no unique factors about location, such as policy effort, that are influencing birthrates in these counties.

Plotting the birthrate values for several industries confirms that birthrates behave in a fairly predictable way from year to year (see Figures 6.9 and 6.10). The plots for each county track each other rather well over time, indicating that these locations are responding in the same way to economic trends that are affecting their behavior.

In contrasts between the levels of birthrates at different sites, Orange

Figure 6.9
Business Services Startups: Growing Counties

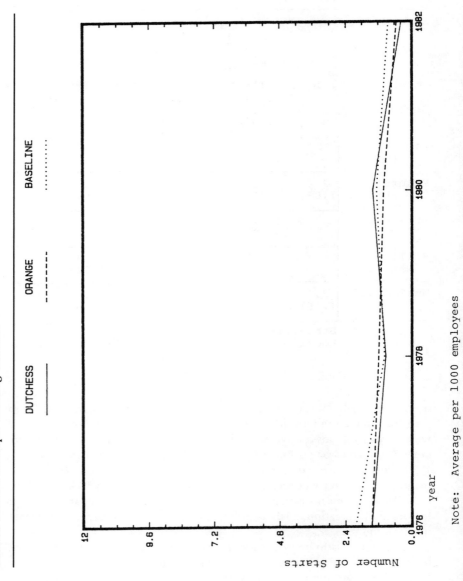

Note: Average per 1000 employees

Figure 6.10
Mature Manufacturing Startups: Growing Counties

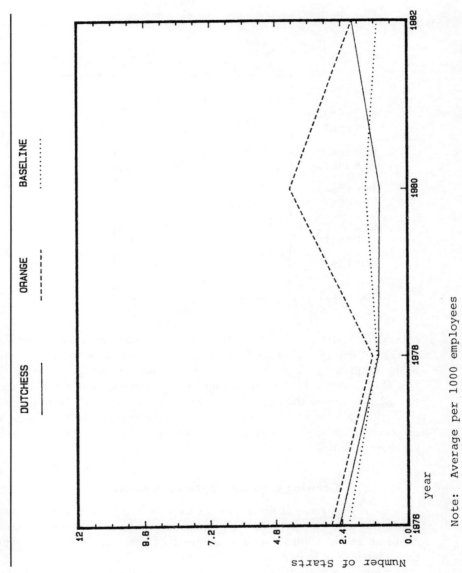

Note: Average per 1000 employees

Table 6.9
Contrast between Mean Birthrates: Dutchess and Orange Counties

	F Value (p <=.10)		
	Orange- Dutchess 1980 1982	Orange- Baseline 1980 1982	Dutchess- Baseline 1980 1982
Bus. Svcs.			
High Tech. Manuf.			
Mature Manuf.	2.9** (.10)	4.1** (.05)	
Personal Svcs.			
Small Firm Manuf.		3.0** (.09)	
Wholes.		4.1** (.05)	

** Orange's birthrate was higher

county birthrates turned out to be significantly different from the baseline average in mature and small firm manufacturing and in wholesaling while being significantly different from Dutchess County's birthrates only in the first of these (see Table 6.9). In no industry was Dutchess County's birthrate significantly higher than Orange's or the baseline counties'. Note too that the high technology SICs, which were identified as being the most likely to respond quickly to shifts in small business policy, show no significant results for these counties.

Growing Counties: Birthrate Change Scores

In the change score analysis, Orange County improved its birthrates significantly more than the baseline counties in mature and small firm manufacturing and in wholesaling but increased its birthrate significantly more than Dutchess only in mature manufacturing (see Table 6.10).

Summing up these findings, Orange performed better than the baseline average in three industries in 1980 and better than Dutchess in only one of these. Its increase in birthrate was higher than those in both Dutchess and the baseline counties in only one industry in one year. This indicates that

Table 6.10
Contrast between Change Scores: Dutchess and Orange Counties

	F Value (p <=.10)					
	Orange-Dutchess		Orange-Baseline		Dutchess-Baseline	
	1978 /80	1980 /82	1978 /80	1980 /82	1978 /80	1980 /82
Business Services						
High Tech. Manuf.						
Mature Manuf.	2.9** (.01)	3.0* (.08)	3.1** (.09)			
Personal Services						
Small Firm Manuf.				2.8** (.10)		
Wholes.				5.3** (.03)		

* Dutchess' increase was steeper
** Orange's increase was steeper

Orange's attempts to advertise its hidden advantages and express its appreciation for business had little impact on entrepreneurs in the years examined here.

SUMMARY

The entrepreneurial model would suggest that Oneida's rather innovative and risk-oriented development effort should significantly increase business startups in a number of industries. This would be especially true of several of the industries examined here, including high technology manufacturing, small firm manufacturing, and business services. The data do not confirm this expectation. In fact, Niagara performed at least as well as Oneida in most of the industry groupings examined here.

As the policy descriptions in Chapter 5 suggest, Orange was not as active or innovative as Oneida in promoting small firms, or in economic development generally. It did take an interesting approach to economic development in that the county executive sought to focus attention on economic development and encourage private-sector initiative without committing many public resources to the development effort. Orange as a whole seemed to be more interested in promoting development than Dutchess and did have more manpower devoted to the effort. Nevertheless, Orange's startup activity was not significantly better than that of Dutchess or the baseline average.

These findings should discourage those who expect to increase the rate of business starts through local policy initiatives alone. A number of possibilities can be suggested for why the more active counties did not see such an increase, and these are discussed in the next chapter.

NOTES

1. Cross-sectional analysis was criticized earlier as being inappropriate where developmental sequences are at work. Its use is justified here because the discussion in the previous chapter leads to specific predictions about where and when differences in mean birthrates are expected to occur.

2. Relatively few firms enter D & B's files immediately after birth. When births are broken down to the three-digit SIC level, as I wanted to do for this research, birth counts are too low to produce much variation between sites. Counting firms zero or one years old in a year as births produces more nonzero cells. An alternative way of counting births would be to take the firms detected by D & B in the year they were born (e.g., firms with business age 0 in 1976) and add the firms that were born in 1976 and detected by D & B within the next two years (i.e., those whose business age was two in 1978 and that were different from the first set of firms). The first method was thought to be less biased in detecting the range of firms born in a particular year. Only about 40 percent of firms survive their first year; those that do may be quite different from those that do not.

3. The employment data come from *County Business Patterns*.

4. In some cases business starts occurred in an industry having fewer than fifty employees, in which case the industry is not reported separately in the data published by the Census Bureau in *County Business Patterns*. When this happened the SIC for that county and year was dropped. This was done for less than 3 percent of the cells.

5. I thank Thomas Rodick and Louis Moon of the New York State Department of Labor for supplying the UI data.

6. The SICs and their respective titles are: 23-Apparel, 27-Printing and Publishing, 30-Rubber, 34-Fabricated Metals, 35-Machinery, 36-Electrical and Electronic Equipment, 38-Instruments, 42-Trucking, 47-Transportation Services, 50-Durable Goods Wholesale, 51-Nondurable Goods Wholesale, 61-Credit Agencies, 62-Security Brokers, 64-Insurance Agents, 65-Real Estate, 73-Business Services, 80-Health Services, 81-Legal Services, 82-Educational Services, 83-Social Services.

7. The assumption behind including this variable was that the matching approach used did not adequately control for all the differences between the sites that might

challenge policy as an explanation for observed differences in birthrates. Policy effort (location) could only be an explanation of birthrate differences if it turned out to be significant in explaining births after controlling for birth levels that occurred before the policy change came about. In practical terms this means that since policy in Oneida and Orange only became more entrepreneurial in 1979 and 1980, it could not explain births in 1978. This approach may underadjust for group differences, which can lead to the conclusion that policy has an impact when no effect actually occurred (Reichardt 1979).

8. Technically, it shows the F score of the between group sum of squares produced by grouping the cases (SICs) into high and low effort and baseline counties while controlling for birthrates in earlier years.

Chapter 7

Reconsidering Entrepreneurial Promotion

STRUCTURING POLICIES AROUND THE ENTREPRENEURIAL ACT

It is widely accepted that government should play an integral part in entrepreneurial development. The assumption is that if government and private interests provide the right kind of supports, more firms will start and survive.

The evidence examined here indicates that activist government has produced neither the positive effects hoped for by its proponents nor the dire consequences predicted by critics of government. Counties that did more to help small firms did not have higher levels of birth activity than counties that did very little. Providing counseling and financing to small business, while helpful to individual small, young firms, has little impact on the business startup rate in either growing or distressed counties. Showing an interest in business, being a cheerleader for private-sector economic development initiatives, or advertising an area's quality of life advantages had no special effect on startup rates in the one county that used this approach in this study. Furthermore, while critics of government activism say that taxes and regulation produce a bad business climate, New York State counties as a whole did surprisingly well at creating new firms when compared to similar counties in Pennsylvania, Ohio, and Michigan. This occurred despite New York's image at the time as a state where the business climate was more anti-business than in most states.

The findings reported here support studies by Carlton, Pennings, and Dennis discussed earlier. Despite the use of different methodologies, the data indicate that the public policy environment is not important in business startup activity when measured at the community or state level.

For anyone involved in the delivery of small-business assistance these findings are rather unbelievable. People working in economic development can point to numerous examples where assisting firms is helpful to the firm and creates jobs. It is useful to consider some of the evidence about small-business assistance to understand the contradictory findings.

Positive Effects of Government Assistance

Allen and Rahman's study (1985) of twelve business incubators located in Pennsylvania concluded that the incubators had a positive effect on firms in them. One-half of the fifty-four firms responding to a survey said that their presence in the incubator affected their business strategy, usually speeding up the pace at which the business plan was implemented. On the other hand, 87 percent of the owners said they would have started their business even if the incubator were not available. The authors concluded that incubators do increase the survival chances of new firms and "yield positive benefits to an area's entrepreneurial climate" (1985, 22).

Studies focusing on small-business counseling available through small-business development centers also report positive effects. Chrisman and others (1985) found a positive benefit-cost ratio between spending for small-business development centers and increased corporate and individual income taxes generated by the firms that had been assisted. Rocha and Khan (1984) followed eighty-four firms that had solicited assistance from the small-business development center at the University of Lowell. Approximately 75 percent of the recommendations put into effect were judged useful by the firms' management. If the advice was implemented within one year its positive effect on firm performance was higher. Three-quarters of managers perceived that their financial position had improved since counseling. Finally, 84 percent wanted to use the services of the center again and 94 percent would recommend the service to others.

Britain's New Enterprise Program has had good results helping entrepreneurs get started (Birley 1985). The program is an intensive educational experience designed to help prospective entrepreneurs develop their business idea, create a viable business plan, and put the plan into action. The program chooses only those who are judged to have the energy and knowledge to run a business, commitment, a viable business idea, openness to learning, and the ability to gather the necessary resources (1985, 8). Of the 263 participants between 1977 and 1981, 96 percent successfully started a venture. Birley contends that many of the businesses would not have been started but for the program. Many of the participants were not traditional entrepreneurial types and lacked a "burning desire for independence," some even feared the idea. Finally, "almost all of the participants started, and are still running independent businesses" (1985, 12).

These studies lead to the conclusion that programs to assist new or small firms do help ventures get under way or improve performance if they are intensive and designed around the needs of a particular group or individual

business. It does not seem, however, that offering policies generally supportive of small firms or even providing counseling to existing small business
somehow causes people in the general community to view the location as
favorable for new firms and convinces them to go ahead with their startup.
In other words if we propose to raise the level of entrepreneurship in the
community we must either engage in support programs on a scale many
times larger than states or communities have tried or we must sharply target
our efforts to carefully selected individuals who are good candidates and
not pretend that we will have a large impact on the general level of entrepreneurship in the community.

This may seem obvious, but many governmental economic development
policies touted as promoting the entrepreneurial climate are little more than
disconnected activities addressed to different types of managerial and operating problems of firms at different stages of the life cycle. If we are serious
about helping entrepreneurs we cannot merely repackage existing development incentives into smaller units or run business startup seminars and
expect to stimulate entrepreneurs to act. Several issues deserve careful attention—-the length of time a program is in effect and the level of support
given to the program; how we believe entrepreneurs make decisions and
what this means for policy design; and how well the mechanisms we use to
carry out policy are adapted to the way the entrepreneur does business.

Searching for the Perfectly Implemented Program

Given the fact that development policy in the more supportive counties
was not dramatically different from policy in the less active counties, some
may argue that more extensive and better-funded efforts would have had an
impact. This is possible, but even if it is true, consider the range of activities
falling under the rubric of "entrepreneurial promotion policy." Fully implementing such an approach places enormous demands on the resources
and personnel in local development organizations. A large number of actions
must be undertaken as a package over an extended period before entrepreneurs not directly touched by the program will notice that the area is "good
for new business." Providing new-business assistance as an adjunct to industrial recruitment had no effect on the birthrates in the counties examined
here. It seems that a critical mass of policies directed just at entrepreneurs
must be available before entrepreneurs begin to take notice.

A related issue is the nature of the policies pursued. For the most part
entrepreneurial development programs use tools government developers are
comfortable with: financing, technical assistance, physical facilities, and information. The more fundamental forces bringing entrepreneurship about,
such as family, the presence and effectiveness of social networks, or attitudes
supportive of entrepreneurship, receive virtually no serious attention from

formal economic development programs. Indeed, we have seen earlier that such forces may lie beyond the influence of any governmental program.

Even if better funding and a more thoroughly implemented entrepreneurial model would produce higher rates of startups, knowing this does not help most communities very much. Not many localities will be able to implement the policy because of its expense and the demands that it places on local development organizations. Few states are likely to be able to extend the approach beyond more than one state-wide program, which would diminish its impact in any one community. Clearly, the entrepreneurial model can only be seriously undertaken in selected (one might say privileged) locations where there is a combination of local initiative, flexible state legislation regarding local autonomy, and available federal, state, and private funding programs to provide operating funds.

Model of Entrepreneurial Decision Making

Entrepreneurs do not seem to respond to moderate levels of entrepreneurial promotion. It may be that our understanding of how entrepreneurs respond to environmental conditions is faulty. Either entrepreneurs do not pay attention to local policy during their startup activity or they do not use information about their environment in the way predicted by the model.

Regarding the first possibility, local government policy is a minor source of uncertainty for the prospective new-business owner when compared to other potential sources such as locating suppliers, identifying markets, and keeping an eye on the competition. Moderately innovative or merely inoffensive local policy may simply be background noise to the entrepreneur scanning his organization's environment for threats or opportunities. Only when local policy deviates beyond some parameters (that probably vary by industry and perhaps by individual) will it be labeled significant and attention given to dealing with its implications. Because local government's powers and resources are limited, they cannot disturb the area's economic climate enough to positively or negatively affect businessmen's startup decisions in any major way.

As to the second possibility, extremely aggressive regulatory or tax policies may scare off potential investors from an area but the reverse does not seem to be true. The more helpful localities in this study did no better at creating new firms than the less aggressive ones. One must even wonder how negative policies must be before businessmen get fed up enough to stop investing, since New York seemed to do well despite its negative image. In short, writers and business lobbyists who argue that this or that set of policies will have either dire or highly favorable consequences on business investment (e.g., McClelland and Magdovitz 1981; Heikoff 1979a) are simply wrong, at least as far as small-business entrepreneurs are concerned.

It is possible that a change in government policy does change the entrepreneur's perception of government. Entrepreneurs were not surveyed directly in this study to see if their perceptions of a locality improved with the more helpful policies. But if their perceptions did change, it had no impact on their behavior because startup rates did not improve in the time covered by this study. Attitudinal changes without behavior change are of little interest to cities concerned about increasing their business activity.

Policy Mechanisms and the Entrepreneurial Style

Entrepreneurial policy is being used as a technical fix for economic development needs. The assumption seems to be: provide certain kinds of services and the population will react to the incremental additions in a rational way. The mechanisms we use to carry out policy and their relationship to the way the entrepreneur does business affect how they are received by entrepreneurs, however. Work by Gasse (1986) suggests that some entrepreneurs are more likely to seek out and use management advice and techniques that might be offered by business assistance programs. Firm age also affects managerial concerns about what government is up to. Managers of younger firms are much more occupied with internal and market affairs. Information search and collection practices become more sophisticated as the firm grows and interacts more intensively with a diversity of outside influences. The population that consumes entrepreneurial assistance not only is likely to be the sort that would use such information anyway but would also put it to more effective use than other types of firms. This points to the fact that even if we could greatly expand business assistance programs, they would not be consumed by all entrepreneurs. Government policy directors need to identify just who the clientele population is and how they will benefit from the services government provides.

THE POTENTIAL FOR PUBLIC IMPACTS

If the entrepreneurial model is to work at all it needs to be fully operational at the community level. The program must be intensive, designed around community needs, managed at the community level, and sustained over a long period of time. While the nature of the important variables in the entrepreneurial startup decision compels action at this level, the practical difficulties of such an undertaking are many. If states and communities are serious about entrepreneurship they might want to consider the following actions.

Community-based Leadership Development. Entrepreneurship is a community and social phenomenon, as well as an economic activity. For too long economic development has been construed narrowly in terms of financial packaging or industrial recruitment. The complexity of the entrepreneurial development approach, and its interconnections with social structures, overwhelm the ability of the traditional leadership structures to drive the process. Few citizens are knowledgeable about the structure of their local economies, what resources and skills are available, or what opportunities exist to make the local economy more creative and vital. If entrepreneurial development is to be more than a token collection of programs, it is imperative that individuals sympathetic to entrepreneurial thinking be spread throughout community structures and organizations, nonprofits, for-profits, and governmental bodies. Leadership training programs under way in many communities get at this need to educate a core of community members about how to identify gaps in programs and policy, seek out solutions, locate resources, and assemble a team to address the problem. We are familiar with the concept of training people to be business entrepreneurs; what is needed is training in the practice of entrepreneurial community policy. Any community that allows professional developers to be completely in charge of development efforts will be unable to do much to promote entrepreneurship.

Community Development versus Economic Development. Economic development promotion is more often concerned about bricks and mortar and jobs than about the nature of the jobs being created or the skill base they are imparting to the community. We have been creating jobs for people or training them to fill available jobs rather than operating from the assumption that any person can create his or her own job through entrepreneurial initiative. As long as entrepreneurship is seen as the province of unique individuals we will not fundamentally change the cultural values needed to support broad-based entrepreneurial initiative. If we are interested in promoting entrepreneurship, jobs and wages are inadequate measures of effectiveness. We have seen that entrepreneurship grows out of a milieu of small firms, a diversity of organizational forms, and a diversity of perspectives, among other factors. The question policy makers need to ask is, what kind of investments do we need to promote that will make our community more able to supply the supports necessary to make entrepreneurship feasible? And more pointedly, are the firms we are helping with our incentives the ones that are most likely to strengthen our community's ability to generate its own firms in the future?

Community Autonomy and Financial Capability. There are a lot of reasons why states thoroughly control the powers available to their local jurisdictions. If communities are to promote entrepreneurship they need flexibility to engage in cooperative ventures with public and private organizations. Sources of funding to support the development effort and to invest in the higher-risk small firm are important, for example. Communities have made innovative use of the CDBG, UDAG, and Economic Development Administration (EDA) programs to establish new-venture financing pools. With the shrinkage of these programs it is important for states to develop replacements or empower their communities to do so. Community taxing and fund-raising are severely limited when the investments are not in physical projects but in risky new ventures. Especially in communities with already weak economies, where entrepreneurship is most needed, local resources cannot be the only source of funding.

There is a trade-off between the feasibility of establishing such programs in a community and the ability of such efforts to show results in the aggregate business activity indicators. There should be no question that intervention will help, if we look at a small enough population, i.e., the single individual or firm. Managerial and financial supports will help a firm get under way and help it be more successful. The problem is in detecting the effects of these efforts in larger population aggregates, such as metropolitan or state levels. The effect of public action is simply overwhelmed by other forces.

There is also a minimum size community where entrepreneurial development policies are likely to be most feasible. Sparse population, limited buying power and market opportunities, mean that starting a firm in small towns or rural areas is more difficult. This is where community entrepreneurship development efforts are most needed. But this is also where initiating and sustaining entrepreneurial development policies is most difficult. Small organizational populations and limited numbers of people with the energy and skills to support entrepreneurial development mean that even offering such policies will be difficult. This is why developing leadership for public policy entrepreneurship is so important.

CONCLUSION

The concept of using entrepreneurship as an economic development tool is an extremely attractive one for policy makers and local communities struggling with issues of jobs and community vitality. It is attractive because it suggests helping the little guy, strengthening community networks, increasing community vitality, and working with local people. Unfortunately our vision of what ought to be helpful to entrepreneur is clearer than our understanding of how the policies should be structured or how to make them work in practice. The first steps have been taken toward developing the correct policies, and this is one of the first efforts to evaluate their impact. The negative findings reported here should neither be dismissed as premature nor taken to indicate that entrepreneurial promotion is never going to produce results. Continued evolution of entrepreneurial development policies will take place regardless of negative findings. However, if we want to avoid putting resources into programs that do little to promote entrepreneurial activity, we need to continually ask critical questions about what it is we expect to accomplish through entrepreneurial development and how to go about it.

Note on the Quasi-Experimental Research Design

Quasi-experimentation is a form of comparative research that strives to inject more rigor into data collection than is usual in comparative studies. It features careful case selection, like the comparative approach, and is most effective where the intervention or stimulus is clearly defined and occurs rapidly. The design's purpose is to make use of naturally occurring "experiments" where the independent variable changes rather abruptly in one or a few sites but not in other similar sites (Campbell and Stanley 1963; Cook and Campbell 1979). The researcher does not actively manipulate the independent variable but can make use of changes brought about for other reasons, often policy interventions. This is the case with small-business development policy which for a number of reasons became more prevalent beginning in 1978 (see Chapter 5).

THE CONTROL SERIES DESIGN

The control series design is an extension of the more familiar interrupted time series design. The interrupted time series design requires that the researcher take observations on the variables of interest before and after the policy intervention occurs. To determine that the intervention caused any fluctuations in the post-intervention observations two questions must be answered. Is the change significantly different from random fluctuations in the series? Is the fluctuation attributable to the intervention? Answering the first question depends on using tests of validity, such as differences of means to test for significance. The second question depends on what other events occurred around the time of the intervention that might have caused the observed deviation. The essence of quasi-experimentation is to set up a clear test of the policy intervention by trying to eliminate other potential explanations of the behavior of the outcome variables.

The single time series design has trouble eliminating rival explanations because one cannot be sure that in unobserved groups the behavior being studied has not deviated in a similar manner even without treatment. The control series design attempts to control for this threat by collecting observations on one or more comparison sites that share characteristics with the test site except that no intervention occurs in them. Assuming that the sites are affected similarly by external factors, the addition of the control series should reveal if external factors are causing fluctuations in the variables of interest. The control series design is most useful in controlling for variables that have similar effects in the cases being examined. According to most observers, a pronounced feature of local economies is that outside forces determine to a great degree their health, job growth, and stability.

In applying the control series design to economic development policy, we must disarm what Campbell and Stanley call "rival hypotheses" that can confound observed relationships between variables of interest. Two types of validity are most important for our purposes. *Internal validity*, which is concerned with whether a causal relationship exists between variables, and *construct validity*, which is about whether the observed variables A and B accurately measure the constructs A and B (Cook and Campbell 1979, 83).

THREATS TO INTERNAL VALIDITY

There are many potential threats to internal validity. Three affect this reseach: history, maturation, and selection.

History. This is a threat "when an observed effect might be due to an event which takes place between the pretest and the posttest, when this event is not the treatment of research interest" (Cook and Campbell 1979, 51).

Business startups increase when the national economy is on the upswing and decrease when the economy is in recession (SBA 1983, 145). Business failures show the opposite behavior, although the business cycle may be only a minor cause in business failures (SBA 1983, 162). In the period under study (1976–1982) the business cycle was rising between 1975 and 1980 and in a downturn between 1980 and early 1983. Business cycle effects would make it harder to find positive effects for policy. National economic trends would promote business startups in the first period where local policies did not yet exist and discourage them during the second period, when we are looking for local policy effects.

Looking at entrepreneurial sites in terms of just their own history would make it hard to determine whether local programs or national trends caused the change in startup rates. To reduce the chances of this occurring, data on a set of baseline counties were assembled to help separate business cycle effects from local policy effects. Mean figures on business births for the set of baseline counties will be compared with the same data for high and low policy effort counties. The level of policy entrepreneurship in baseline counties is unknown. Nevertheless, assuming that some are active and others are not, the effects of local policy will cancel themselves out if mean figures on business activity across these counties are used.

Business cycles do not cause equally rapid increases or decreases in business activity in different locations. A primary determinant of these time delays is the makeup of the local economic base. Areas with large percentages of manufacturing employment are more sensitive to business cycle changes than are areas dominated by service or retailing firms. Unfortunately, there is little evidence to show how an area's economic base conditions the response of firm births to business cycle changes. Areas with similar economies are expected to respond in roughly similar ways to business cycles. To show whether business cycles are affecting births in the areas being examined, they will be matched with similar counties, and changes in firm birthrates over the course of the business cycle will be examined. If local development policies are helping startups, the test counties should display higher birthrates regardless of the business cycle trend.

Maturation. This is a threat when natural changes at the site make the area more able to produce firms, without appreciable inputs from public policy. This is the problem Pennings's study (1982b) encountered by examining older industrial SMSAs and growing Sunbelt SMSAs at one point in time. The threat of maturation is addressed in this study by concentrating on Northeastern counties where natural economic evolution is likely to have similar effects on the birth potential of the area between the mid–1970s and the early 1980s.

Selection. This potentially serious threat is seen "when an effect may be due to the difference between the kinds of people in one experimental group as opposed to another" (Cook and Campbell 1979, 53). The basic design of this research is to pick several counties that have adopted a number of entrepreneurial policies and compare the birthrates in them to other counties where governments have not been as entrepreneurial. Selection simply means that there may be something unique about the entrepreneurial counties that not only causes the governments to adopt innovation but also causes more entrepreneurs to start businesses in them.

Selection is likely to understate rather than overstate the impact of entrepreneurial policy. Counties whose local economies are seriously depressed may try to promote entrepreneurs as a way to revitalize themselves. Counties that are growing probably would not bother with explicit small-firm policies because the costs are too high and the payoffs too precarious. This threat is partly addressed by comparing entrepreneurial and non-entrepreneurial counties that have similar levels of economic health. In other words, an entrepreneurial, but depressed, county is compared to another depressed county, not to a rapidly growing one.

There is another aspect to this threat that cannot be addressed by case selection. Since counties with weak economies are more likely to use entrepreneurial policies, the impact of such policies may be small since the adopters are starting from a weak initial position. If no impact is found it may still be that in healthier localities the policies might have useful impacts on business births. What this means is simply that the findings can only be generalized to counties similar to those that have adopted entrepreneurial policies. Other research (probably using experimentation) will be needed to see what effects entrepreneurial policies induce in healthier economies.

CONSTRUCT VALIDITY

This refers to the possibility that the "operations which are meant to represent a particular cause or effect construct can be construed in terms of more than one construct" (Cook and Campbell 1979, 59). One important threat to validity is of special concern in attempting to measure local public policies: the confounding of a construct with levels of the construct. In Cook and Campbell's words:

One might conclude from an experiment that A does not affect B when in fact A-at-level-one does not affect B, whereas A-at-level-four might well have affected B if A had been manipulated as far as level four. (1979, 67)

Business development policies available for study at the time this research was conducted were not particularly entrepreneurial. Local governments operating within the existing policy framework (i.e., level-one implementation) cannot have as large an impact on births as when they have available new state and national policies giving them more appropriate resources (level-four implementation). This factor will reduce the observed impact of development policies on startup rates in the locations examined.

Development Organizations in Study Sites

AGENCIES

Oneida

Mohawk Valley Economic Development District (MVEDD) An agency funded by the U.S. Economic Development Administration to promote economic development in a seven-county region including Oneida County. Its primary mechanisms are public works grants, planning assistance grants, and loan packaging for businesses.

Oneida County Industrial Development Corporation (OCIDC) A private, non-profit Local Development Corporation (LDC) organized to promote business in Oneida County. It was organized in 1962 and annually receives approximately 50 percent of its operating budget from the county.

Rome Industrial Development Corporation (RIDC) An LDC organized in the mid–1960s to develop and sell space in an industrial park developed in the city of Rome. It is staffed by the Rome Chamber of Commerce on a part-time basis and has served as a conduit for SBA 502 and 503 money as well as New York State JDA monies.

Utica Economic Reinvestment Program (UERP) Program administered by the Utica Department of Urban and Economic Development. Established in 1978, four full-time staff administer a loan, grant, and public works program funded by Community Development Block Grant monies allocated to it by the city.

Niagara

Niagara County Department of Economic Development and Planning An arm of Niagara County government, this seven-person department's economic development responsibilities include research, grant preparation, and tourist promotion.

Niagara County Industrial Development Authority (NCIDA) A two-person office organized as an arm of the legislature and partially funded by the county until recently. It is the primary development arm of the county, and its main form of assistance is the IRB.

Niagara Falls Department of Economic Development Created in 1981 and staffed by the City of Niagara Falls to administer its $1.2 million revolving loan program that used CDBG funds as seed money. Its major project has been a large shopping mall in the downtown area which was completed in 1982.

Orange

Orange County Industrial Development Authority (OrCIDA) A local development organization with a board of directors appointed by the county executive to issue industrial revenue bonds. OrCIDA has a part-time attorney whose time and staff work are reimbursed by the Authority from the fees it charges for granting approval of revenue bonds.

Orange County Chamber of Commerce (Middletown) An active chamber covering the middle portion of the county. There is a friendly rivalry with the East Orange Chamber for recruiting firms and undertaking development promotion activities. The chambers are the most active bodies in contacting external and local firms about their needs.

East Orange County Chamber of Commerce (Newburgh) Like the Orange County Chamber this chamber has been active on development issues. Its director and several staff people have been active in assembling loan packages for expanding businesses in the Newburgh area.

Newburgh Economic Development Agency Created by the City of Newburgh in 1981, this is the only local development agency in the county that serves as a one-stop facility that can also provide its own financing. The city has programs aimed at minority businesses, expanding local firms, and external firms considering Newburgh for a plant site.

Orange County Economic Development Committee Organized at the initiative of the county executive in 1978, this group consists of elected officials and administrators, representatives of chambers of commerce, banks, and area employers. Its main purpose is to improve the flow of communication between these public and private individuals and organizations and to provide a forum for working on joint projects. It has no staff or budget of its own.

Private Industry Council A successor to the Comprehensive Employment and Training Act programs aimed at job training. Government and business representatives sit on the board of directors and allocate federal funds coming into the community under the program for salary subsidies for workers undergoing on-the-job training, for studies pertaining to economic development concerns, and for recruiting new businesses.

Dutchess

Dutchess County Economic Development Corporation (DCEDC) A local development corporation organized in 1978 and funded in part by county and municipal governments and in part by businesses. Its three professional staff members recruit firms to the county and assist established local firms in assembling financing and locating suitable facilities.

Poughkeepsie Area Chamber of Commerce This chamber is involved in providing information to prospective firms, representing the commercial interests in the local community, and providing the business perspective on transportation, housing, and quality of life issues on the local agenda.

LOCAL CAPITAL PROGRAMS

Revolving Loan Funds (RLFs) These are funds administered locally to provide low-interest, subordinated debt for construction, rehabilitation, equipment, and working capital. The seed funds come from CDBG loan repayments (UERP), allocations from a city's CDBG entitlement (UERP, RIDC), federal agency grants (MORECO), and county grants (OCJDLF).

Oneida

MORECO (Mohawk Valley Rehabilitation Corporation)
$800,000
UERP (Utica Economic Reinvestment Program)
$900,000
RERP (Rome Economic Reinvestment Program)
$500,000
OCJDLF (Oneida County Job Development Loan Fund)
$500,000

Niagara

NFLDC (Niagara Falls Local Development Corporation)
$1,200,000

Orange

Newburgh City Revolving Loan Fund
$600,000
Newburgh Minority Venture Capital Loan Fund
$130,000

OTHER CAPITAL SOURCES

New York State Job Development Authority (JDA) A state agency authorized to sell up to $300 million in general obligation bonds for the purposes of reloaning the monies at below-market rates for buildings, and equipment associated with new or expanding operations in manufacturing, commercial, or pollution control facilities. Local Development Corporations administer the application process at the local level.

Small Business Guaranteed Loan Programs Include the 90 percent bank guarantee program, and SBA 502 and 503 programs. The latter two were designed to allow LDCs to apply for special SBA loans and then reloan these to businesses.

Industrial Revenue Bonds (IRBs) Municipal bonds that exempt buyers from federal and New York State income taxes and permit lower than market rates of interest to the borrower. Can be used for land, buildings, and equipment by firms engaged in manufacturing, warehousing, research, or commercial activities.

Questionnaire Used in the Study

COUNTY: _____   DATE: _____

INFORMANT: _____   TIME: _____

ORGANIZATION: _____   TEL: _____

In this survey three terms have particular meanings

Small/New Firm:
   —independent, that is not a branch or subsidiary of a larger firm
   —usually smaller than 20 employees
   —less than 5 years old

Established Firm:
   —any firm in the community longer than 5 years

Municipality:
   —city, town, or village governments

1. Some people say that the rate at which small businesses are started in an area is influenced by how willingly governments in the area work in partnership with the business community. "Willingness to work with" implies things such as being able to cut red tape and respond quickly to requests for zoning changes, or with information on sites, services, regulatory or tax policies. It also suggests that elected and appointed officials are open to small business's point of view and when differences arise, actively work with businesses to find solutions.

   First, as to the importance of local government policy in a businessman's choice of location. Would you say that policies followed by local governments?

   _____ Influence a good number of small business location decisions?

   _____ Influence some small business location decisions?

   (OR)

_____ Influence very few small business location decisions?

2. Have government officials in the larger municipalities in the county initiated many development projects designed to improve the local economy or have they tended to follow the private sector's lead?

3. Below are listed nine types of actions that governments sometimes take to improve the local economy. Please indicate whether or not municipal governments in your county or the county itself have used the policy that you know of.

Yes   No

Has the county or any municipality:

_____ _____ Coordinated improvements in streets, sewerage or other public services with private improvements taken by businesses?

Has the county or any municipality:

_____ _____ Contacted businesses in the county through surveys or on-site visits to uncover problems which local governments may help solve?

_____ _____ Participated in committees whose purpose was to improve communication between business and government or solve mutual problems?

_____ _____ Helped firms with fewer than 20 employees to acquire loans through industrial revenue bonding, or private sources such as banks?

_____ _____ Reduced or simplified local regulatory permits, inspections, or paperwork required of firms?

_____ _____ Assisted in recycling abandoned industrial or commerical properties into space for small or new firms?

_____ _____ Assigned a person to troubleshoot problems with commercial or industrial projects arising out of local regulatory procedures? Example: zoning, building codes, licenses, or environmental clearances.

_____ _____ Made a practice of providing to new local businesses information on specialized business services available locally, such as financial, engineering, consulting, or advertising services?

_____ _____ Tried to motivate banks or local investors to set up a private revolving loan fund to invest in new or expanding local businesses?

4. Businessmen sometimes complain about the way government treats them. Cited are things such as delays in making decisions, unreasonable tax assessments, or unduly strict regulations. In your judgement what legitimate complaints are made about the way local governments in your area go about their regulatory, taxing, or service providing activities?

5. Local governments try in various ways to improve their economies. Sometimes policies of this sort are cited by business or government as having made a significant impact on the local economy. What specific county or municipal actions do you think have had the most POSITIVE impact on small firms in the county in the last 5 years?

6. Four types of firms that you may deal with on various matters are listed below.

After reading the list, please rank them from 1–4 in order of how much time you spent working with such firms in the last 3 months.

(1)received most of your attention and (4) least.

_____ Established local firms over 5 years old.

_____ Firms based outside the community interested in moving a branch or other facility into the area.

_____ Firms that have indicated they may leave the area.

_____ Small/New firms.

7. Below are listed types of information and resources that some researchers say owners of new small firms often need but cannot readily locate on their own. 129ease indicate if new small firms come to you for such assistance OFTEN, SOMETIMES, or HARDLY EVER.

	OFT	ST	H E
Information about sites and buildings available in the local area	___	___	___
Help in settling problems they may have with building and fire codes, licenses or permits, or zoning regulations	___	___	___
Capital for structures or equipment	___	___	___
Working capital	___	___	___
Information about potential private investors	___	___	___
Help in generating information about local or regional markets for their products or services	___	___	___
Help in dealing with state or federal agencies	___	___	___
Help in getting public functions near their locations improved, e.g., streets, sidewalks, sewerage, parking	___	___	___

8. What are the primary objectives of your organization on economic development matters? Have you targeted particular industries or job categories for special emphasis?

9. How long have you been active in economic development in your county?

10. Names and positions of others familiar with how development programs operate in your area.

Cluster Map of Baseline Counties

ALLIN   Allen, IN
ATLNJ   Atlantic, NJ
BEAPA   Beaver, PA
BRONY   Broome, NY
BUTOH   Butler, OH
BUTPA   Butler, PA
CALMI   Calhoun, MI
CAMPA   Cambria, PA
CHAIL   Champaign, IL
CHANY   Chautauqua, NY
CLAOH   Clark, OH
DUTNY   Dutchess, NY
GLONJ   Gloucester, NJ
JACMI   Jackson, MI
KALMI   Kalamazoo, MI
KANIL   Kane, IL
LACPA   Lackawanna, PA
LAKOH   Lake, OH
LEHPA   Lehigh, PA
LOROH   Lorain, OH
MADIL   Madison, IL
MAHOH   Mahoning, OH
MUSMI   Muskegon, MI
NIANY   Niagara, NY
NORPA   Northampton, PA
ONENY   Oneida, NY
ORANY   Orange, NY
OTTMI   Ottawa, MI
PEOIL   Peoria, IL
RENNY   Rensselaer, NY

ROCNY   Rockland, NY
SAGMI   Saginaw, MI
SOMNJ   Somerset, NJ
STCIL   St. Clair, IL
STJIN   St. Joseph, IN
TRUOH   Trumbull, OH
ULSNY   Ulster, NY
VANIN   Vander, IN
WASMI   Washtenaw, MI
WASPA   Washington, PA
WINIL   Winnebago, IL

Appendix D
Cluster Map of Baseline Counties

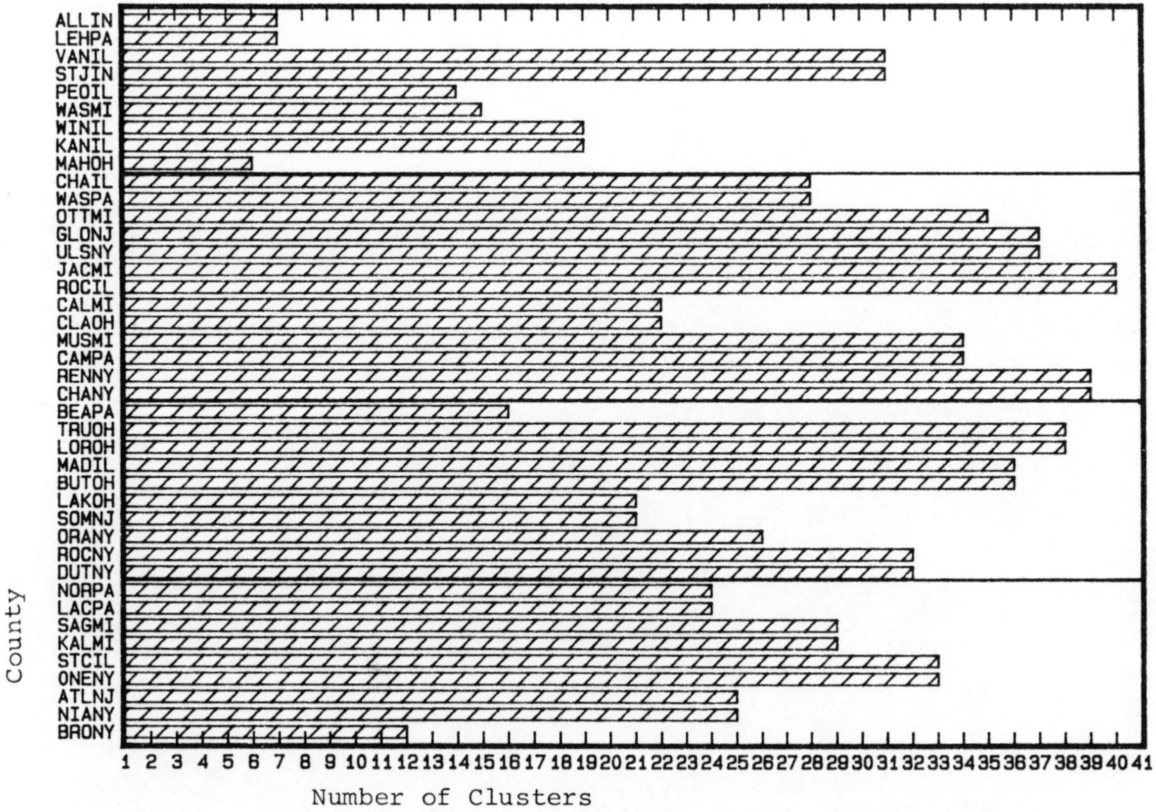

County
ALLIN
LEHPA
VANIL
STJIN
PEOIL
WASMI
WINIL
KANIL
MAHOH
CHAIL
WASPA
OTTMI
GLONJ
ULSNY
JACMI
ROCIL
CALMI
CLAOH
MUSMI
CAMPA
RENNY
CHANY
BEAPA
TRUOH
LOROH
MADIL
BUTOH
LAKOH
SOMNJ
ORANY
ROCNY
DUTNY
NORPA
LACPA
SAGMI
KALMI
STCIL
ONENY
ATLNJ
NIANY
BRONY
1 2 3 4 5 6 7 8 9 10 11 12 13 14 15 16 17 18 19 20 21 22 23 24 25 26 27 28 29 30 31 32 33 34 35 36 37 38 39 40 41
Number of Clusters

Note: Procedure identified four groups of Counties

Industries Used in the Study

Standard Industrial Classification three-digit code in parentheses.

MANUFACTURING INDUSTRIES

High Technology Industries

Engines/Turbines (351)

Construction Equipment (353)

Metalworking Machinery (354)

General Industrial Machinery (356)

Office/Computing Machinery (357)

Electrical Transmission Equipment (361)

Radio/TV Receiving Equipment (365)

Electronic Components and Assembly (367)

Engineering/Laboratory Instruments (381)

Measuring and Controlling Devices (382)

Optical Instruments/Lenses (383)

Medical/Dental Equipment (384)

Photographic Equipment (386)

This list of industries comes from Glasmeier, Markusen, and Hall (1983) and is based on the percentage of engineers, scientists, and mathematicians employed in the industry.

Small Firm Industries

Commercial Printing (257)

Miscellaneous Plastic Products (307)

Heating Equipment (343)

Fabricated Structural Metals (344)

Garden Machinery (352)

Construction, Mining and Material Handling Equipment (355)

Miscellaneous Machinery, Except Electrical (359)

These industries have 60 percent or more of their employees working in firms of less than 500 employees (U.S. SBA, 1984).

Mature Manufacturing

Includes all of the small business industries above except for commercial printing and miscellaneous plastic products plus:

Cutlery, Handtools and General Hardware (342)

Refrigeration and Service Industry Machinery (358)

Household Appliances (363)

Electric Lighting and Wiring Equipment (364)

SERVICE INDUSTRIES

All service industries were identified from J. C. Burrows, C. E. Metcalf, and J. B. Kaler, *Industrial Location in the United States* (Lexington, Mass.: Heath Lexington Books, 1971); T. M. Stanback et al., *Services: The New Economy* (Totowa, N.J.: Allanheld, Osmun and Co., 1981); and T. M Stanback, *Understanding the Services Economy: Employment, Productivity, Location* (Baltimore: Johns Hopkins University Press, 1979).

Business Services

Trucking (421)

Public Warehousing (422)

Business Credit Institutions (615)

Mortgage Bankers and Brokers (616)

Security Brokers, Dealers and Flotation Companies (62)

Insurance Agents, Brokers and Services (641)

Other Business Services (73)

Legal Services (811)

Personal Services

Arrangement of Transportation (472)

Savings and Loans (612)

Personal Credit Institutions (614)

Offices of Physicians (801)

Dentists (802)

Other Health Practitioners (804)

Medical and Dental Laboratories (807)

Correspondence, Vocational, and Schools not elsewhere classified (82)

Vocational Rehabilitation Services, Child Day Care, Residential Care Facilities, Social Services not elsewhere classified (83)

These industries were selected because they are oriented to local markets. They would be responsive to changes in the economic health of a locality, which might happen if government development efforts were very successful.

Wholesaling

Motor Vehicles (501)

Furniture (502)

Metals and Minerals (505)

Electrical Goods (506)

Hardware and Plumbing and Heating (507)

Machinery, Equipment and Supplies (508)

Paper and Paper Products (511)

Drugs, Drug Proprietaries (512)

Groceries (514)

Chemicals and Allied Products (516)

Beer, Wine, and Distilled Alcoholic Beverages (518)

These industries were chosen because they are oriented to exporting from the local area and do not depend on the economic health of the immediate area to the same degree as other industries. They might therefore be able to respond rapidly to changes in local economic policy even if the local market area is still depressed.

References

Advisory Commission on Intergovernmental Relations (ACIR). 1967. State-local taxation and industrial location. *Report A–30.* Washington, D.C.: U.S. GPO.
———. 1978. State mandating of local expenditures. *Report A–67.* Washington, D.C.: U.S. GPO.
———. 1980. Regional growth: Historic perspective. *Report A–74.* Washington, D.C.: U.S. GPO.
———. 1981a. Measuring local government discretionary authority. *Report M–131.* Washington, D.C.: U.S. GPO.
———. 1981b. Regional growth: Interstate tax competition. *Report A–76.* Washington, D.C.: U.S. GPO.
———. 1981c. The states and distressed communities. *Report M–133.* Washington, D.C.: U.S. GPO.
———. 1982. State and local roles in the federal system. *Report A–88.* Washington, D.C.: U.S. GPO.
AFSCME (American Federation of State, County and Municipal Employees) study shows five-year decline in grant-in-aid funding. 1986. *Federal Grants Management Handbook* (November): 3–4.
Alabama Business Research Council. 1970. *Industrial development bond financing: Business and community experiences and opinions.* University, Alabama: University of Alabama Press.
Aldrich, H. E. 1979. *Organizations and environments.* New York: Prentice-Hall.
Aldrich, H. E., B. Rosen, and W. Woodward. 1986. Social behavior and entrepreneurial networks: Summary. In *Frontiers of entrepreneurship research.* Ed. R. Ronstadt, J. Hornaday, R. Peterson, and K. Vesper, 239–40. Wellesley, Mass.: Center for Entrepreneurial Studies, Babson College.
Aldrich, H. E., and C. Zimmer. 1986. Entrepreneurship through social networks. In *The art and science of entrepreneurship.* Ed. D. L. Sexton and R. W. Smilor, 3–24. Cambridge, Mass.: Ballinger Publishing Company.
Allen, D. N., and S. Rahman. 1985. Small business incubators: A positive environment for entrepreneurship. *Journal of Small Business Management* (July): 12–22.

Apilado, V. P. 1971. Corporate-government interplay: The era of industrial aid finance. *Urban Affairs Quarterly* 7 (December): 219–41.

Armington, C., and M. Odle. 1982. Sources of job growth. *Economic Development Commentary* (Fall): 3–7.

Arthur D. Little, Inc. 1981. Industrial Marketing Program: Orange County, New York. Cambridge, Mass. Mimeo.

Aulde, A. J. 1980. *The effectiveness of state and local industrial development incentives*. Occasional Paper 10. Program in Urban and Regional Studies, Cornell University, Ithaca, New York, August.

Balderston, K. M. 1986. *Plant closings, layoffs, and worker readjustment: The states' response to economic change*. Washington, D.C.: National Governors' Association, Center for Policy Research and Analysis. July.

Bardach, E. 1977. *The implementation game*. Cambridge, Mass.: MIT Press.

Baumol, W. J. 1983. Toward operational models of entrepreneurship. In *Entrepreneurship*. Ed. Joshua Ronen, 29–48. Lexington, Mass.: Lexington Books.

Bearse, P. 1976. Government as innovator: A new paradigm for state economic development policy. *New England Journal of Business and Economics* 2 (Spring): 37–57.

———. 1984. An econometric analysis of black entrepreneurship. In *Frontiers of entrepreneurship research*. Ed. J. A. Hornaday, F. Tarpley, Jr., J. A. Timmons, and K. H. Vesper, 212–31. Wellesley, Mass.: Center for Entrepreneurial Studies, Babson College.

Bearse, P., and D. Konopko. 1979. A comparative analysis of state programs to promote new technology-based enterprise. *New England Journal of Business and Economics* (Spring): 49–74.

Beaumont, E. F., and H. A. Hovey. 1985. State, local and federal development policies: New federal patterns, chaos, or what? *Public Administration Review* (March/April): 327–32.

Begley, T. M., D. P. Boyd. 1986. Psychological characteristics associated with entrepreneurial performance. In *Frontiers of entrepreneurship research*, 146–65. See Aldrich, Rosen, and Woodward 1986.

Ben-Chieh, L. 1975. *Quality of life indicators in the U.S. metropolitan areas, 1970*. Kansas City, Mo.: Midwest Research Institute.

Birch, D. 1979a. *The job generation process*. Cambridge, Mass.: MIT Program on Neighborhood and Regional Change.

———. 1979b. Testimony on the job generation process. In U.S. Congress, Joint Economic Committee, The Effective Utilization of Small Business to Promote Economic Growth, Hearing, October 25, 1979, 96th Congress, 1st Session.

Birley, S. 1984. New firms and job generation in St. Joseph County. In *Frontiers of entrepreneurship research*, 232–48. See Bearse 1984.

———. 1985. Encouraging entrepreneurship: Britain's new enterprise program. *Journal of Small Business Management* (October): 6–12.

———. 1986. The small firm: Set at the start. In *Frontiers of entrepreneurship research*, 267–80. See Aldrich, Rosen, and Woodward, 1986.

Bowen, D. D., and R. D. Hisrich. 1986. The female entrepreneur: A career development perspective. *Academy of Management Review* 11, no. 2: 393–407.

Bozeman, B., and J. L. Bozeman. 1987. Manufacturing firms' views of government activity and commitment to site: Implications for business retention policy. *Policy Studies Review* 6, no. 3: 538–53.

Braden, P. 1977. *Technological entrepreneurship*. Ann Arbor, Mich.: Division of Research, Graduate School of Business, University of Michigan.

Brittain, J. W., and J. H. Freeman. 1983. Et tu brute: Individual mobility and population proliferation. Paper presented at the annual meeting of the Academy of Management, Dallas, Texas, August 14–17.

Brockhaus, R. H., Sr. 1982. The psychology of the entrepreneur. In *Encyclopedia of entrepreneurship*. Ed. C. Kent, D. A. Sexton, and K. Vesper, 39–56. Englewood Cliffs, N.J.: Prentice-Hall Inc.

Brockhaus, R. H., Sr., and P. S. Horwitz. 1986. The psychology of the entrepreneur. In *The art and science of entrepreneurship*, 25–48. See Aldrich and Zimmer 1986.

Brockhaus, R. H., Sr., and W. R. Nord. 1979. An exploration of factors affecting the entrepreneurial decision: Personal characteristics vs. environmental conditions. *Academy of Management Proceedings*, 39th Annual Meeting, Atlanta, Georgia, August 8–11, 1979.

Bruno, A. V., and T. Tyebjee. 1982. The environment for entrepreneurship. In *Encyclopedia of entrepreneurship*, 288–306. See Brockhaus 1982.

Bryce, H. J., ed. 1979. *Revitalizing cities*. Lexington, Mass.: Lexington Books.

Burns, T., and G. M. Stalker. 1961. *The management of innovation*. London: Tavistock Publications.

Burrows, J., C. Metcalfe, and J. Kaler. 1971. *Industrial location in the United States*. Lexington, Mass.: D.C. Heath.

Butler, S. 1981. *Enterprise zones: Greenlining the inner city*. New York: Universe Books.

Cameron, G. C. 1980. The inner city: New plant incubator. In *The inner city: Employment and industry*. Ed. A. Evans and D. Eversley, 351–66. London: Heineman.

Campbell, D. T., and J. C. Stanley. 1963. *Experimental and quasi-experimental designs for research*. Chicago: Rand McNally.

Carlton, D. W. 1979. Why new firms locate where they do: An econometric model. In *Interregional movements and regional growth*. Ed. W. C. Wheaton, 13–50. Washington, D.C.: The Urban Institute.

Carroll, G. R., and Y. P. Huo. 1986. Organizational task and institutional environments in ecological perspective: Findings from the local newspaper industry. *American Journal of Sociology* 91: 838–73.

Carsrud, A. L., C. M. Gaglio, and K. W. Olm. 1986. Entrepreneurs: mentors, networks, and successful new venture development: An exploratory study. In *Frontiers of entrepreneurship research*, 229–35. See Aldrich, Rosen, and Woodward.

Carsrud, A. L., K. W. Olm, and G. G. Eddy. 1986. Entrepreneurship: Research in quest of a paradigm. In *The art and science of entrepreneurship*, 367–78. See Aldrich and Zimmer 1986.

Charles River Associates, Inc. 1976. *An analysis of venture capital market imperfections: Prepared for the National Bureau of Standards, Experimental Technology Innovation Program*. Cambridge, Mass.

Chinitz, B. 1979. An historical perspective: Small business development in region

II. In *The environment for entrepreneurship and small business.* U.S. Small Business Administration. Washington, D.C.: U.S. GPO.

Chrisman, J. J., R. R. Nelson, F. Hoy, and R. B. Robinson, Jr. 1985. The impact of SBDC consulting activities. *Journal of Small Business Management* (July): 1–11.

Clarke, M. 1987. Competing in a global economy. *Governors' Weekly Bulletin* 11 (March 13): 42–44.

Conference report: Taxable financing urged as alternative to tax-exempt bonds. 1986. *Report on Development Financing* (March 3): 4–7.

Cook, T. D., and D. T. Campbell. 1976. The design and conduct of quasi-experiments and true experiments in field settings. In *Handbook of industrial and organizational research.* Ed. M. D. Dunnette, 223–326. Chicago: Rand McNally.

———. 1979. *Quasi-experimentation: Design and analysis issues for field settings.* Boston: Houghton Mifflin.

Cooper, A. C. 1971. Technical entrepreneurship: What do we know? *R & D Management* 3: 59–64.

———. 1984. Contrasts in the role of incubator organizations in the founding of growth-oriented firms. In *Frontiers of entrepreneurship research*, 159–74. See Bearse 1984.

Coopers and Lybrand Economic Studies Group. 1982. Impact of enterprise zone tax incentives on selected small businesses. U.S. Department of Housing and Urban Development, Washington, D.C.

Cornia, G., W. A. Testa, and F. D. Stocker. 1978. *State-local fiscal incentives and economic development.* Columbus, Ohio: Academy for Contemporary Problems.

Council for Northeast Economic Action. 1980. *Local economic development: Public leveraging of private capital.* Boston, Mass.

County Business Patterns. See U.S. Department of Commerce, Bureau of the Census.

Crisafulli, V. C. 1960. *An economic analysis of the Utica-Rome area.* Utica, N.Y.: The Utica College Research Center, Syracuse University.

Cross, M. 1981. *New firm formation and regional development.* Westmead, Farnborough, Hants, England: Gower Publishing Co. Ltd.

Daniels, B., and M. Kieschnick. 1978. *Theory and practice in the design of development finance innovations.* Washington, D.C.: U.S. Dept. of Commerce, Economic Development Administration.

Danielson, M. H., and J. W. Doig. 1982. *New York: The politics of urban regional development.* Berkeley: University of California Press.

Dennis, W. T. 1986. Explained and unexplained differences in comparative state business starts and start rates. In *Frontiers of entrepreneurship research*, 313–27. See Aldrich, Rosen, and Woodward.

Dickson, P. R., and J. Giglierano. 1985. Missing the boat and sinking the boat: A new model of entrepreneurial risk. Working Paper Series, College of Administrative Science, The Ohio State University.

Doctors, S. T., and R. E. Wokutch. 1983. The importance of state and local government assistance to small business development. *Public Administration Quarterly* 7 (Spring): 76–90.

Dommel, P. R. 1982. *Decentralizing urban policy: Case studies in community development*. Washington, D.C.: Brookings.

———. 1984. Local discretion: The CDBG approach. In *Urban economic development*. Ed. R. Bingham and J. Blair, 101–13. *Urban Affairs Annual Reviews* Vol 27, Beverly Hills, Calif.: Sage.

Downs, A. 1978. Political interaction is a key ingredient for successful urban investment. *The Mortgage Banker* (April): 62–65.

Drucker, P. 1985. *Innovation and entrepreneurship: Practice and principles*. New York: Harper and Row.

Due, J. F. 1961. Studies of state and local tax influences on the location of industry. *National Tax Journal* 14 (June): 163–73.

Duncan, R. B. 1972. Characteristics of organizational environments and perceived environmental uncertainty. *Administrative Science Quarterly* no. 3: 313–27.

Epstein, N. 1987. It works, but don't call it industrial policy. *Washington Post National Weekly Edition*, January 12: 25.

Erdevig, E. A. 1986. Small business, big job growth. *Economic Perspectives, The Federal Reserve Bank of Chicago* x, no. 6: 15–24.

Eulau, H., and K. Prewitt. 1973. *Labyrinths of democracy*. Indianapolis: Bobbs-Merrill.

Fagg, J. J. 1980. A reexamination of the incubator hypothesis: A case study of greater Leicester. *Urban Studies* 17 (1980): 35–44.

Fennell, M. A. 1980. The effects of environmental characteristics on the structure of hospital clusters. *Administrative Science Quarterly* 25, no. 3 (September): 485–510.

Fenstermaker, V. 1972. *Sources of equity capital used by new and small business firms in Louisiana, Arkansas, Mississippi, and Tennessee*. Chapel Hill, North Carolina: Institute of Applied Business and Economic Research, University of North Carolina.

Finnerty, J. F., and A. T. Krzystofik. 1985. Barriers to small business formation. *Journal of Small Business Management* (July): 51–58.

Ford, J. D., and J. W. Slocum. 1977. Size, technology, environment and the structure of organizations. *Academy of Management Review* (2): 561–75.

Freiser, J. 1982. The urban development action grant program. In *Mobilizing capital*. Ed. Peter Bearse. New York: Elsevier.

Frug, G. E. 1980. The city as legal concept. *Harvard Law Review* 93, no. 6: 1059–1154.

Garfield-Schwartz, G. 1979. The scope for local government action. In *Central city economic development*. Ed. Benjamin Chinitz, 161–74. Cambridge, Mass.: Abt Books.

Gartner, W. B. 1984. Problems in business startup: The relationships among entrepreneurial skills and problem identification for different types of new ventures. In *Frontiers of entrepreneurship research*, 496–512. See Bearse 1984.

———. 1985. A conceptual framework for describing the phenomenon of new venture creation. *Academy of Management Review* 10 (October): 696–706.

Gasse, Y. 1986. The development of new entrepreneurs: A belief-based approach. In *The art and science of entrepreneurship*, 49–60. See Aldrich and Zimmer 1986.

Gatewood, E., F. Hoy, and C. Spindler. 1984. Functionalist vs. conflict theories:

Entrepreneurship disrupts the power structure in a small southern community. In *Frontiers of entrepreneurship research*, 265–79. See Bearse 1984.

Gellman Research Associates, Inc. n.d. *The relationship between industrial concentration, firm size and technology innovation*. Washington, D.C.: U.S. Small Business Administration.

Gibbs, J. P., and D. L. Poston, Jr. 1975. The division of labor: Conceptualization and related measures. *Social Forces* 53 (March): 468–75.

Gillespie, D. F., and D. S. Mileti. 1977. Technology and the study of organizations: An overview and appraisal. *Academy of Management Review* 2: 7–16.

Glasmeier, A. K., A. R. Markusen, and P. G. Hall. 1983. *Defining High Technology Industries*. Working Paper No. 407. Berkeley, Calif.: University of California, Institute of Urban and Regional Development.

Gold, R. B. 1966. Subsidies to industries in Pennsylvania. *National Tax Journal* 19 (September): 286–97.

Gollub, J., and S. A. Waldhorn. 1980. *Rediscovering governance: Using non-service approaches to strengthen small business*. Menlo Park, Calif.: Center for Public Policies and Analysis, SRI International.

Goodman, R. 1979. *The last entrepreneurs: America's regional wars for jobs and dollars*. New York: Simon and Schuster.

Govindarajan, V. 1984. Managerial characteristics and organizational environment: A contingency approach. Working Paper Series, College of Administrative Science, The Ohio State University.

Gray, J. C., and D. A. Spina. 1980. State and local industrial location incentives— A well-stocked candy store. *The Journal of Corporation Law* (Spring): 520–690.

Greene, R. 1982. Tracking job growth in private industry. *Monthly Labor Review* 105, no. 4 (September): 3–9.

Greenwood, M. J. 1981. *Migration and economic growth in the U.S.: National, regional, and metropolitan perspectives*. New York: Academic Press.

Gudgin, G. 1978. *Industrial location processes and regional employment growth*. Westmead, Farnborough, Hants, England: Saxon House.

Hagen, E. E. 1975. *The economics of development*. Rev. ed. Homewood, Ill.: Richard Irwin.

Hannan, M. T., and J. H. Freeman. 1977. The population ecology of organizations. *American Journal of Sociology* 82: 929–64.

Hansen, D. 1979. Banking and the finance of small business. Working Paper. Washington, D.C.: Council of State Planning Agencies.

Harris, C. 1981. A comparison of employment data for several business data sources: *County Business Patterns*, Unemployment Insurance, and the Brookings' U.S. Establishment and Enterprise Microdata File. Washington, D.C.: The Brookings Institution, Working Paper No. 5. Mimeo.

———. 1982. U.S. establishment and enterprise microdata: Database description. Business microdata project. Washington, D.C.: The Brookings Institution. Mimeo.

———. 1984. The magnitude of job loss from plant closings and the generation of replacement jobs: Some recent evidence. *The Annals of the American Academy of Political and Social Science* 475 (September).

———. n.d. Methodological differences in job generation studies of David Birch and of Catherine Armington and Margie Odle, Washington, D.C.: Brookings Institution. Mimeo.

Harrison, B., and S. Kanter. 1978. The political economy of states' job-creation business incentives. *American Institute of Planners Journal* (44): 424–35.

Hart, S. L., and D. R. Denison. 1987. Creating new technology-based organizations: A system dynamics model. *Policy Studies Journal* 6 (3): 512–28.

Hebert, R., and A. Link. 1982. *The entrepreneur: Mainstream views and radical critiques.* New York: Praeger.

Heikoff, J. M. 1979. *Management perceptions of the business climate in New York State.* Graduate School of Public Affairs, Albany: State University of New York.

Heikoff, J. M., C. Wissel, C. Wesley, and W. V. Kasson, Jr. 1979. *Urban economic development: A peek into the literature.* Albany, N.Y.: Center for Government Research and Services, SUNY-Albany.

Hellman, D. A., G. H. Wassall, and L. H. Falk. 1976. *State financial incentives to industry.* Lexington, Mass.: Lexington Books.

Herzik, E. B., and J. P. Pelissero. 1986. Decentralization, redistribution and community development: A reassessment of the small cities CDBG program. *Public Administration Review* 46, no. 1: 31–37.

HUD. See U.S. Department of Housing and Urban Development.

Increase the odds. 1986. *Economic Growth and Revitalization Report* (November 11): 3.

Incubator without walls. 1986. *Economic Growth and Revitalization Report* (December 23): 5–6.

Jacobs, J. 1979. Are business incentives doing their job? *Journal of Housing* (36): 504–12.

———. 1984. *Cities and the wealth of nations: Principles of economic life.* New York: Random House.

Jarret, J. 1979. *Creating jobs: Connecticut's Product Development Corporation.* Lexington, Ky., The Council of State Governments.

Jennings, D. E., and C. P. Zeithaml. 1983. Locus of control: A review and directions for entrepreneurial research. *Academy of Management Proceedings*, 43rd Annual Meeting, Dallas, Tex., August 14–17, 1983: 417–21.

Johnson, J. M. 1979. Determinants of unsuccessful risk capital funding by small business. *American Journal of Small Business* 4 (July): 31–38.

Johnson, P. S., and D. G. Cathcart. 1979. The founders of new manufacturing firms: A note on the size of incubator plants. *Journal of Industrial Economics* (28): 219–24.

Kazanjian, R. K. 1984. Operationalizing stage of growth: An empirical assessment of dominant problems. In *Frontiers of entrepreneurship research*, 144–58. See Bearse 1984.

Kent, C. A., D. A. Sexton, and K. Vesper, eds. 1982. *Encyclopedia of entrepreneurship.* Englewood Cliffs, N.J.:Prentice-Hall Inc.

Kieschnick, M. 1979. *Venture capital and urban development.* Washington, D.C.: Council of State Planning Agencies.

Kieschnick, M., L. Litvak, and B. H. Daniels. 1980. *Financing new business development.* Washington, D.C.: Council of State Planning Agencies.

Kilby, P. 1971. *Entrepreneurship and economic development*. New York: The Free Press.

Kirzner, I. M. 1979. *Perception, opportunity and profit*. Chicago: University of Chicago Press.

Kleinbaum, D. G., and L. L. Kupper. 1978. *Applied regression analysis and other multivariate methods*. North Scituate, Mass.: Duxbury Press.

Laird, W. E., and J. R. Rinehart. 1974. Are local industrial promotion efforts self-regulating? *AIDC Journal* 9 (3): 61–75.

Ledebur, Larry, and William W. Hamilton. 1986. The great tax-break sweepstakes *State Legislatures* (September): 12–15.

Levy, J. M. 1981. *Economic development programs for cities, counties, and towns*. New York: Praeger.

Lewis, C. W., and M. J. Tenzer. 1985. Community collaboration: Public-private partnerships in Connecticut. Presented at the Annual Meeting of the American Political Science Association, New Orleans, Louisiana, August 29-September 1.

Lijphart, A. 1971. Comparative politics and the comparative method. *American Political Science Review* 65 (3): 682–93.

Lincoln, J. R. 1979. Organizational differentiation in urban communities: A study in organizational ecology. *Social Forces* 57: 915–30.

Lipset, S. M., and W. Schneider. 1987. The confidence gap during the Reagan years, 1981–1987. *Political Science Quarterly* 102, no. 1: 1–24.

Lipsky, M. 1980. *Street-level bureaucracy*. New York: Russell Sage Foundation.

Litvak, L., and B. Daniels. 1979. *Innovations in development finance*. Washington, D.C.: Council of State Planning Agencies.

Long, W., and W. E. McMullin. 1984. Mapping the new venture identification process. In *Frontiers of entrepreneurship research*, 567–91. See Bearse 1984.

Lovell, C. 1981. Evolving local government dependency. *Public Administration Review* Special Issue (January): 189–202.

Major provisions of the Tax Reform Act of 1986. 1986. *Congressional Quarterly Weekly Report* (October 4): 2350–2358.

Malizia, E. E. 1986. Economic development in smaller cities and rural areas. *Journal of the American Planning Association* 52 (Autumn): 489–99.

Malizia, E. E., and S. Rubin. 1985. A grass roots development strategy with local development organizations. *Rural Development Perspectives* (June): 7–13.

Marrett, C. B. 1980. Influences on the rise of new organizations: The formation of women's medical societies. *Administrative Science Quarterly* 25: 185–99.

Massey, J., and J. D. Straussman. 1985. Another look at the mandate issue: Are conditions-of-aid really so burdensome? *Public Administration Review* 45 (2): 292–300.

McClelland, P. D., and A. L. Magdovitz. 1981. *Crisis in the making: The political economy of New York State since 1945*. Cambridge, England: Cambridge University Press.

McClintock, C. C., D. Brannon, and S. Maynard-Moody. 1979. Applying the logic of sample surveys to qualitative case studies: The case cluster method. *Administrative Science Quarterly* 24: 612–29.

McHone, W. 1984. State industrial development incentives and employment growth in multistate SMSAs. *Growth and Change* (October): 8–15.

MDC, Inc. 1986. *Shadows in the sunbelt: Developing the rural south in an era of economic change.* A Report of the MDC Panel on rural economic development. Chapel Hill, N.C.

Metcalfe, J. 1967. War between the states: Developers open fire in battle to attract new industries. *Magazine of Wall Street* 119 (February 18): 26–29.

Meyer, J. W., and B. Rowan. 1977. Institutionalized organizations: Formal structure as myth and ceremony. *American Journal of Sociology* 83: 340–63.

Meyer, M., and Associates. 1978. *Environment and organizations: theoretical and empirical perspectives.* San Francisco: Jossey-Bass Inc.

Middletown Times Herald Record. May 30, 1971, May 5, Nov. 29, 1972, Jan. 24, 1973, May 14, 1973, Aug. 19, 1979, Sept. 15, 1980, Feb. 17, 1981. Middletown, New York.

Mid-Hudson Patterns for Progress, Inc. 1983. The Mid-Hudson: New York's natural growth area. Vol. 1, *Economic resources inventory.* Prepared for Central Hudson Gas and Electric Corporation. Poughkeepsie, N.Y.

Midwest Research Institute. 1986. *A rural economic development source book: Selected training and technical assistance materials.* Kansas City, Mo.

Miles, M. B. 1979. Qualitative data as an attractive nuisance: The problem of analysis. *Administrative Science Quarterly* 24: 590–601.

Miller, J. P. 1985. Rethinking small businesses as the best way to create rural jobs. *Rural Development Perspectives* (February): 9–12.

Mokry, B. 1985. The birth of small business organizations: The impact of capital, technical assistance and political climate. Ph.D. diss., Syracuse University, Syracuse, N.Y.

Molotch, H. 1976. The city as a growth machine: Toward a political economy of place. *American Journal of Sociology* (September): 309–32.

Morgan, W. E., and M. M. Hackbart. 1974. An analysis of state and local industrial tax-exemption programs. *Southern Economic Journal* 41 (October): 200–205.

Morrison, J. n.d. *Small business: New directions for the 1980s.* Washington, D.C.: National Center for Economic Alternatives.

Morrison, P. 1978. New York State's transition to stability: The demographic outlook. In *The declining Northeast: Demographic and economic analyses.* Ed. B. Chinitz. New York: Praeger.

Mt. Auburn Associates. 1986. Designing a state small business incubator policy. *The Entrepreneurial Economy* (November): 1–13.

National Association of Towns and Townships. 1985. *Harvesting hometown jobs.* Washington, D.C.: National Association of Towns and Townships.

National Institute for Advanced Studies. 1978. Public/private strategies for involving small business in community economic revitalization: A policy-oriented analysis. *Final Report,* HUD, Office of Economic Affairs.

National Tax Association, Committee on Intergovernmental Fiscal Relations. 1968. Property taxation and interstate competition for industry. *Proceedings of the Sixtieth Annual Conference on Taxation.* Columbus, Ohio.

Newburgh Evening News. Aug. 9, 1982. Newburgh, New York.

New York State Assembly, Office of the Speaker. 1980. *Small business: New York's forgotten majority.* Albany, N.Y.

New York State, Department of Commerce. 1980. Personal income in areas and counties of New York State. *Research Bulletin No. 48.* Albany, N.Y.

New York State Legislature, Commission on Expenditure Review. 1974. Industrial development in New York State, Program Audit 12.1.74. Albany, N.Y.

New York State Legislature, Assembly, Committee on Oversight, Analysis and Investigation. 1981. *New York State industrial development agencies: The objectives in 1967, the reality of 1981.* Albany, N.Y.

New York State Legislature, Commission on State-Local Relations. 1983. *New York's local government structure: The division of responsibilities: An interim report.* Albany, N.Y.

New York State, Science and Technology Foundation. 1983. *1981–1982 Report.* Albany, N.Y.

New York State, SUNY, Albany. 1983. *1983–84 New York State statistical yearbook.* Albany: Nelson Rockefeller School of Government and Public Affairs.

Niagara Falls Gazette Apr. 19, 1972, Mar. 30, 1980, Mar. 7, 14, 1981. Niagara Falls, New York.

Patterson, D. J. 1967. The local industrial development corporation. *Research Report No.5* Bloomington: Indiana University, Bureau of Business Research, Graduate School of Business.

Pelissero, J. P. 1986. Intrametropolitan economic development policies: An exploratory look at suburban competition and cooperation. Presented at the Midwest Political Science Association Annual Meeting, Chicago, Illinois, April 10–12.

Pennings, J. M. 1982a. The urban quality of life and entrepreneurship. *Academy of Management Journal* 25: 63–79.

———. 1982b. Organizational birth frequencies: An empirical investigation. *Administrative Science Quarterly* 27: 120–44.

———. 1982c. Elaboration on the entrepreneur and his environment. In *Encyclopedia of entrepreneurship,* 307–12. See Brockhaus 1982.

Pennsylvania's decline will be minimal in 1986 IDB allocation. 1986. *Report on Development Financing* (January 20): 7–9.

Peterson, P. E. 1981. *City limits.* Chicago: University of Chicago Press.

Peterson, R., and N. R. Smith. 1986. Entrepreneurship: A culturally appropriate combination of craft and opportunity. In *Frontiers of entrepreneurship research,* 1–11. See Aldrich, Rosen, and Woodward.

Peterson, R. A. 1980. Entrepreneurship and organization. In *Handbook of organization design.* Ed. P. Nystrom and W. Starbuck, 65–83. Oxford: Oxford University Press.

Pfeffer, J., and G. R. Salancik. 1978. *The external control of organizations.* New York: Harper and Row.

Pierce, N. R., and C. Steinbach. 1981. Reindustrialization on a small scale—But will the small business survive? *National Journal* (January 17): 105–8.

Pilcher, D. 1986. Old term has new meaning. *State Legislatures* (August): 18–21.

Porter, M. E. 1986. States expect to lose under tax reform. *Local/State Funding Report* 15 (45): 4–5.

Poughkeepsie Journal. Aug. 20, 1973, Nov. 19, 1978. Poughkeepsie, New York.

Pratter, J. S., and J. F. Niles. 1980. Local incentives can work. *Economic Development Commentary* 4 (October): 19–23.

Private Sector Initiatives. 1979. *The impacts of government requirements on small business in Washington State.* Seattle, Wash.

Pulver, Glen C. 1986. Community economic development strategies. Publication G3366. Madison: University of Wisconsin Extension Service.

Randolph, W. A., and G. G. Dess. 1981. The relationships among organization environment, technology, structure and performance: A conceptual integration and proposed research procedure. *American Institute for Decision Sciences Proceedings*, Vol. 2.

Redburn, S. 1977. Responding to the industrial decline of America. *Urbanism Past and Present* (Winter): 37–42.

Reichardt, C. S. 1979. The statistical analysis of data from nonequivalent control group designs. In *Quasi-experimentation: Design and analysis issues for field settings*. Ed. T. D. Cook and D. T. Campbell, 147–206. Boston: Houghton Mifflin.

Rocha, J. R., and M. R. Khan. 1984. Assessing counseling efforts for small business operations. Presented at the Annual Meeting of the Northeast Business and Economics Association. Boston, Mass., November 8–9.

Rubin, H. J. 1985. Organization theory and community economic development. Paper presented at the Annual Meeting of the American Political Science Association, New Orleans, Louisiana, August 29-September 1.

Salamon, L., and M. S. Lund. 1984. *The Reagan presidency and the governing of America*. Washington, D.C.: The Urban Institute.

SAS Institute. 1982. *SAS users guide: statistics*. Cary, N.C.: SAS Institue.

Sazama, G. W. 1970. A benefit-cost analysis of a regional development incentive: State loans. *Journal of Regional Science* 10 (3): 385–96.

SBA. See U.S. Small Business Administration.

Schere, J. L. 1982. Tolerance of ambiguity as a discriminating variable between entrepreneurs and managers. *Proceedings of the National Academy of Management*, 404–8.

Schmenner, R. 1980. Industrial location and urban management. In *The prospective city*. Ed. Arthur P. Solomon, 446–68. Cambridge, Mass.: MIT Press.

Schroeder, L., and P. Blackley. 1979. State and local government locational incentive programs. In *The environment for entrepreneurship and small business in region II*. U.S. Small Business Administration. Washington, D.C.: U.S. GPO.

Schumpeter, J. 1934. *The theory of economic development*. Cambridge: Harvard University Press.

Schwartz, R. G., and R. D Teach. 1984. Primary issues affecting the development and growth of a professional infrastructure for emerging technology start-ups: The State of Georgia experience. In *Frontiers of entrepreneurship research*, 126–35. See Bearse 1984.

Seley, J. 1981. Targeting economic development: An examination of the needs of small businesses. *Economic Geography* 57: 35–51.

Sexton, D. L., and N. B. Bowman. 1984. Personality inventory for potential entrepreneurs: Evaluation of a modified JPI/PRF-E test instrument. In *Frontiers of entrepreneurship research*, 513–28. See Bearse 1984.

Shapero, A. 1981. Entrepreneurship: Key to self-renewing communities. *Economic Development Commentary* 7 (April): 19–23.

Shapero, A., and M. Sokol. 1982. The social dimensions of entrepreneurship. In *Encyclopedia of entrepreneurship*. See Brockhaus 1982.

Special Report—States venturing into venture capital: Opportunity or problem? 1983. *Venture Capital Journal* (September): 7–14.

SRI International. 1985. *Financing innovation in enterprise: Beyond venture capital.* Menlo Park, Calif.: SRI International.

Stanback, T. M. 1979. *Understanding the service economy: Employment, productivity, location.* Baltimore: Johns Hopkins University Press.

Stanback, T. M. et al. 1981. *Services: The new economy.* Totowa, N.J.: Alanheld, Osman and Co.

Star, A. D., and C. L. Narayana. 1983. Do we really know the number of small business starts? *Journal of Small Business Management* (October): 44–48.

States take lead in promoting economic change. 1986. *Governors' Weekly Bulletin* September 12.

Stephens, G. R. 1974. State centralization and the erosion of local autonomy. *Journal of Politics* 36, (no. 1): 44–76.

Stinson, T. F. 1968. The effects of taxes and public financing programs on local development. Agriculture Economics Report No. 113. Washington, D.C.: Economic Research Service.

Stober, W. J., and L. H. Falk. 1969. The effect of financial inducements on the location of firms. *Southern Economic Journal* 36, 1: 25–35.

Stonecash, J. 1985. Paths of fiscal centralization in the American states. *Policy Studies Journal* 13, 3: 653–61.

Storey, D. J. 1982. *Entrepreneurship and the small firm.* London: Croom Helm.

Tassey, G. 1977. The effectiveness of venture capital markets in the U.S. economy. *Public Policy* 25, no. 4: 479–97.

Teitz, M. B., A. Glasmeier, and D. Svensson. 1981. Small business and employment growth in California. Working Paper No. 348. Berkeley, Calif.: Institute of Urban and Regional Studies.

Timmons, J. A. 1986. Growing up big: Entrepreneurship and the creation of high-potential ventures. In *The art and science of entrepreneurship*, 223–39. See Aldrich and Zimmer 1986.

Tomaskovic-Devey, D., and S. M. Miller. 1982. Recapitalization: The basic U.S. urban policy of the 1980s. In *Urban policy under capitalism.* Ed. N. Fainstein and S. Fainstein, 23–42. Beverly Hills, Calif.: Sage.

Ungson, G. R., C. James, and B. H. Spicer, 1985. The effects of regulatory agencies on organizations in wood products and high technology/electronics industries. *Academy of Management Journal* 28, no. 2: 426–45.

U.S. Congress, House Committee on Small Business. 1978. Subcommittee on Antitrust, Consumers, and Employment. Future of small business in America. *Report No. 95–1810.*

U.S. Congress, House Committee on Small Business. 1980. Delegate recommendations, White House conference on small business. 96th Congress, 2d Session. Committee Print.

U.S. Congress, Joint Economic Committee. 1979. The effective utilization of small business to promote economic growth. 96th Congress, 1st Session, Oct. 25, 1979. Hearing.

U.S. Department of Commerce, Bureau of the Census. 1972. *County business patterns.* Washington, D.C.: U.S. GPO.

———. 1977. *County business patterns.* Washington, D.C.: U.S. GPO.

————. 1981. *County business patterns*. Washington, D.C.: U.S. GPO.

U.S. Department of Commerce, Bureau of Industrial Economics. 1982. *1982 U.S. industrial outlook*. Washington, D.C.: U.S. GPO.

U.S. Department of Housing and Urban Development (HUD). n.d. *Emerging partnership opportunities for cities*. Prepared with the Economic Development Administration and the Urban Land Institute. Washington, D.C.: U.S. GPO.

U.S. Department of Housing and Urban Development. 1980. *Fifth Annual Community Development Block Grant Report*. Washington, D.C.: U.S. Department of Housing and Urban Development, Office of Planning and Development.

U.S. General Accounting Office. 1981. Small businesses are more active as inventors than as innovators in the innovation process. *Report to the Chairman, Committee on Small Business*. U.S. House of Representatives, PAD 82–19.

U.S. Small Business Administration (SBA). 1982. *The state of small business: A report of the President transmitted to the Congress, March 1982*. Washington, D.C.: U.S. GPO.

————. 1983. *The state of small business: A report of the President transmitted to the Congress, March 1983*. Washington, D.C.: U.S. GPO.

————. 1984. *The state of small business: A report of the President transmitted to the Congress, March 1984*. Washington, D.C.: U.S. GPO.

————. 1986. *The state of small business: A report of the President transmitted to the Congress*. Washington, D.C.: U.S. GPO.

Utica Observer-Dispatch. Apr. 10–11, May 22, Aug. 26, 1974. Jan. 17, 1981. Utica, New York.

Vaughan, R. 1979. *State taxation and economic development*. Washington, D.C.: Council of State Planning Agencies.

————. 1981. State tax incentives: How effective are they? In *Expanding the opportunity to produce*. Ed. R. Friedman and W. Schweke, 260–65. Washington, D.C.: Corporation for Enterprise Development.

————. 1986. *Financing economic development in the south: Public infrastructure and entrepreneurship. 1986 Commission on the Future of the South*. Chapel Hill, N.C.: Southern Growth Policies Board.

Vaughan, R., R. Pollard, and B. Dyer. 1984. *The wealth of states: Policies for a dynamic economy*. Washington, D.C.: Council of State Planning Agencies.

Vesper, K. H. 1980. *New venture strategies*. Englewood Cliffs, N.J.: Prentice-Hall.

————. 1983. *Entrepreneurship and national policy*. Chicago, Ill.: Walter E. Heller Corporation Institute for Small Business.

Webber, M. J. 1972. *Impact of uncertainty on location*. Canberra: Australian National University Press.

Wheat, L. F. 1973. *Regional growth and industrial location: An empirical viewpoint*. Lexington, Mass.: Lexington Books.

Wholey, D. R., and J. W. Brittain. 1986. Organizational ecology: Findings and implications. *Academy of Management Review* 11, no. 3: 513–33.

Widner, R. 1980. City development strategies for the future. In *Cities and firms*. Ed. H. J. Bryce, 195–202. Lexington, Mass.: Lexington Books.

Wilken, P. H. 1979. *Entrepreneurship: A comparative and historical study*. Norwood, N.J.: Ablex Publishing Corp.

Williams, O. P., and C. R. Adrian. 1963. *Four cities: A study in comparative policy making*. Philadelphia: University of Pennsylvania Press.

Yin, R. K. 1981. The case study crisis: Some answers. *Administrative Science Quarterly* 26: 58–65.

Young, E. C., and H. P. Welsch. 1983. Information source selection patterns as determined by small business problems. *American Journal of Small Business* 7, no. 4: 42–48.

Zimmerman, J. F. 1981a. The discretionary authority of local governments. *Urban Data Services Reports* 13, no. 11.

———. 1981b. *The government and politics of New York State*. New York: New York University Press.

———. 1983. *State-local relations: A partnership approach*. New York: Praeger Publishers.

INTERVIEWS CONDUCTED BY AUTHOR

Dutchess County

Bernstein, George, Business Editor, Poughkeepsie Journal, 12/15/83.

Bersak, David, Planning Department, City of Poughkeepsie, 5/25/83.

Fallon, Joan, Director, Southern Dutchess Chamber of Commerce, Beacon, 5/24/83.

Howe, Bert, Director, Dutchess County Economic Development Corporation, Poughkeepsie, 5/19/83, 12/16/83.

McEnroe, Jack, President, Dutchess Bank, Board Member Dutchess County Economic Development Corporation, Poughkeepsie, 12/15/83.

Mitchell, Dick, Director, Poughkeepsie Area Chamber of Commerce, 5/20/83.

Sherman, Jonah, Board Member, Dutchess County Economic Development Corporation, Poughkeepsie, 12/14/83.

Niagara County

D'Attillio, Richard, Niagara County Industrial Development Authority, Lockport, 7/28/83.

Kinyon, Dave, Eastern Niagara Chamber of Commerce, Lockport, 7/28/83.

Mathiasen, Glen, Niagara County Department of Planning and Economic Development, Lockport, 7/27/83, 10/25/83.

McCoy, Robert, Niagara Falls Area Economic Development Agency, 7/27/83, 10/26/83.

Orr, John, Niagara County Savings Bank, Niagara Falls, 10/26/83.

Stamm, Mike, Niagara County Industrial Development Authority, Lockport, 6/3/83, 10/2/83.

Oneida County

Conover, Ronald, Rome Department of Planning and Development, 8/24/83.

Houseknecht, Michael, Utica Department of Urban and Economic Development, 9/20/83.

Ladd, John, Mohawk Valley Economic Development District, 6/1/83, 8/25/83.

Morris, Roger, Oneida National Bank, Utica, 9/14/83.

Potocki, Roger, Oneida County Industrial Development Corporation, 7/29/83, 8/17/83.

Ratazzi, Edward, Rome Industrial Development Corporation, 6/1/83, 9/6/83.

Seidel, David, Utica Economic Revitalization Program, 10/4/83.

Orange County

Boyd, William, Mid Hudson Patterns for Progress, Inc., Poughkeepsie, 6/1/83.

Cosgrove, Dennis, Supervisor, Town of Walkill, 1/4/84.

DeTurk, Richard, Department of Planning and Economic Development, Orange County, 5/3/83, 1/13/84.

Heimbach, Louis, County Executive, Orange County, 1/13/84.

Hellstrom, Carl, Supervisor, Town of Montgomery, 1/14/84.

Holley, Henry, Administrative Director, Orange County Industrial Development Authority, 1/5/84.

Marsh, Dan, Director, Office of Economic Development, City of Newburgh, 5/24/83, 1/3/84.

Novesky, Neil, Assistant Director, Office of Economic Development, City of Newburgh, 1/3/84.

Sullivan, Michael, Orange County Chamber of Commerce, Middletown, 5/31/83.

Taxter, Paul, East Orange Chamber of Commerce, Newburgh, 5/24/83, 5/31/83, 7/27/84.

Index

A. D. Little Company, 73, 74

Baseline counties, 52
Birch, David, 3–4
Business, state and local tax burden, 6
Business incorporations, U.S., 6
Business incubators, 26, 110
Business startup: agglomeration economies and, 19; compared to plant location decision, 32; decision to undertake, 15; desirability and feasibility of, 18–19; in distressed counties, 89–98; ecological structure and, 19, 21; effect of policy climate on, 45–47; government capital assistance to, 25; government strategy to promote, 23–25; in growing counties, 99–105; impact of local policy on, 76–77; local resource base and, 20; measuring, 47, 79–80, 90, 98, 106 n.2; rate, definition, 2, 10 n.2; rate, in U.S., 13–14; social networks and, 22; uncertainty surrounding, 22. *See also* Economic development; Entrepreneur

Capital, resource for business startup, 20
Carlton, Dennis, 45
Case study counties, 51–52; similarities and differences, 60

Community Development Block Grant, 37, 40; benefit to low and moderate income individuals, 43 n.4; used in revolving loan fund, 66
Community leadership, importance in entrepreneurial promotion, 113–14
Connecticut Product Development Corporation, 26
County Business Patterns: data on business starts, 80

Dennis, William T., 47
Dillon's rule, 33
Dun and Bradstreet Corporation, date on business starts, 81–89, 106 n.2
Dutchess County, New York: economic changes 1967–77, 55–60; economic development activities, 70–71; financial assistance to small firms, 69. *See also* Poughkeepsie, New York
Dutchess County Economic Development Corporation, 71

Ecological niche, 19
Economic development: compared to other government services, 35; growth theories, 9; as local political issue, 31–33; methods to promote, 35–41; state spending on, 2; through

About the Author

BENJAMIN W. MOKRY is presently working as a senior planner in the Governor's Office of Federal-State Programs, Department of Planning and Policy, State of Mississippi. In the past he has worked for the Internal Revenue Service and has contributed to *Public Administration Survey* and *Mississippi's Business*.